Birmingham Museums and Art Gallery
in association with Lund Humphries

Michael Rowe

Richard Hill
and Martina Margetts

Birmingham Museums and Art Gallery
Chamberlain Square
Birmingham B3 3DH
www.bmag.co.uk

in association with

Lund Humphries
Gower House
Croft Road
Aldershot
Hampshire GU11 3HR

and

Suite 420
101 Cherry Street
Burlington
VT 05401
USA

www.lundhumphries.com

Lund Humphries is part of Ashgate Publishing

British Library Cataloguing-in-Publication Data
A catalogue record for this book is available from the British Library

ISBN 0 85331 886 7

Library of Congress Control Number: 2003104039

Designed by Chrissie Charlton & Company
Project management by Simon Perry
Typeset by Tom Knott
Printed in Singapore under the supervision of MRM Graphics Ltd

frontispiece
1 Michael Rowe 2002
Photograph: Marc Burden

Contents

Introduction

2 **Box** 1977
Brass, green patination
28 x 15 x 17 cm; 11 x 6 x 6.75 in
Collection: Crafts Council, London
Photograph: Ian Haigh

Modernist principles came late to the applied arts in Britain. That they came to fine metalwork at all is largely due to the work and influence of Michael Rowe. For more than 30 years his concerns to return to essentials, to seek a new vocabulary of form and ornament, and to take silversmithing forward as a valid form of expression have informed both international critical debate and metalwork practice. His role as Senior Tutor at the Royal College of Art has enabled him to inspire an entire generation of craft practitioners.

Rowe makes work that is of great aesthetic power, charged with meaning. It is endlessly readable. The intellectual rigour with which his works are constructed is matched by his technical mastery of metalsmithing to create works that are held in a beautiful tension: between structural theory and sensual surface; between technical perfection and poetic resonance.

However, he is not a prolific maker. His works are, as he admits, 'hard won'. In spite of his vessels being held in public and private collections around the world, they are not always readily visible. This book, together with the retrospective exhibition with which its publication coincides, is therefore all the more timely. It offers the most comprehensive review of Rowe's work to date, as well as providing the first opportunity to see his new body of silver vessels. I hope that it will serve not only to introduce the outstanding work of one of the most influential artists in metal of the past half century to a wide public, but also act as a celebration of Rowe's continuing achievement.

Martin Ellis (Curator, Applied Art)
Birmingham Museums and Art Gallery

Strangely familiar
Martina Margetts

3 **Bowl** 1980
925 silver, copper
10 x 28 x 21 cm; 4 x 11 x 8.25 in
Collection: 401½ Collection
Photograph: Ian Haigh

Singular achievement comes into being in unlikely places and unexpected ways. In the 1960s, at a small technical high school in southern England, two students became friends. Humour and enthusiastic discussions about ideas underpinned the friendship. Over 30 years on, we have seen the flowering productivity of Michael Rowe, silversmith, and Terry Pratchett, novelist. The juxtaposition of their work – enigmatic three-dimensional containers and Brobdingnagian fantasy prose – galvanises curiosity as to what experiences and preoccupations have had a bearing on the development of Rowe's 'project'.[1]

The conjunction of Rowe and Pratchett in those mid-teenage days is not in fact surprising: 'We were both oddballs' says Rowe (an independent stance important for Rowe's career), and while the latter 'devoured *Lord of the Rings* whole', Rowe was responding to the 'very magical thing of making something in metal'. Pratchett's witty drawing of Rowe in a 'Wagnerian Valhalla' was apposite: 'I was steeped in all that' says Rowe – the alchemical and mythological world of making in metal.

The passion Rowe has for working in metal is hard to articulate in words: it is there in the work. Tactile qualities are important but the visual quality is even more so: 'Making perfect things in metal is a wonderful thing; it never leaves you.' The skill and precision is at such a virtuoso pitch in Rowe's work that messages and meanings are always eloquently embodied. The writings of Gaston Bachelard (1884–1962), perhaps more than any others', explore the power of metal and its poetic resonance.[2] Metal has multivalent qualities, but for Rowe form generation relies especially on metal's constructional and surface precision. And this perfecting of form in metal is predicated on the act of drawing and on geometrical analysis, both of which Rowe developed early in his life.

At home, Rowe and his older brother were 'always encouraged to draw', working on huge sheets torn into four from the drawings of his architect father, who also 'drew wonderfully well'. Their parents enthusiastically supported their involvement in art and later, when Rowe discovered an interest in metalwork at school, encouraged them to set up workshop spaces

12

in the garage – a metalworking lathe, woodworking lathe and a pottery wheel for his mother – and there Rowe began to develop his 'metal turn of mind'.

Rowe had 'instantly fallen in love with metalwork' and chose a technically based rather than classical academic education. He considered a career as an engineer, but instead focused his attention from these teenage years on drawing and making with metal: 'Quickly I was finding very interesting things in metalwork. I was also rather good at technical drawing; I saw the connections.' Aged 16, Rowe's drawing master asked him to make a geometric model and presciently Rowe created a model of two intersecting cones out of sheets of brass. Its unusual form and beautiful craftsmanship prompted the headmaster to keep it for display in his office.

Rowe decided to study Art, Engineering Drawing and Metalwork at A-level, an unprecedented choice: 'I got my way and I was a one-man class doing these subjects.' Inspired by his brother's experience of art school, Rowe looked to that kind of future, and at this point a mentor and teacher entered his life in the way that Rowe himself later has entered the lives of so many of his students: 'Graham Arthur is a real influence in my past. A kind and generous man, he let me come and do evening classes to do metalwork. He could see that I had a real obsession with metal. He also had a passion for metal. He was unpedantic and encouraged me to let designs evolve from working processes, always seeking the essentials in a design. This set the path conceptually, breaking things down to fundamentals – that has always been a fascination.'

The union of conceptual rightness and perfect construction is in all Rowe's work. This is perfection founded on the handmade, not on machine precision. His continuous investigation of geometry is a visual proposition. Looking now at the new work, he says again: 'I am always asking myself what are the visual dynamics at work here.'

silver holloware, box, bowl, vase, etc., represented by the basic geometrical solids – the cube, hemisphere and cone – and proposes his own grammar of transformations to generate new forms and attribute meanings in a pure and authentic way. First principles and underlying structures are important because any authenticity and truth in how we perceive the world and organise experience are predicated on the very nature and character of the verbal – and visual – languages themselves.

So, for example, to understand a poem – or an object by Rowe – it is less important to ask what it is about than to contemplate the abstract structures that inform it. By extension, Barthes decoded mass media and popular culture, suggesting they were part of a system of signs, signifiers of meaning. This semiological approach included all objects, so Rowe's work, for example, can be read as an exemplar of encoded meaning while at the same time itself seeking to start from fundamentals and to structure meaning free from the habits of cultural conditioning. The structural laws of language that predetermine meaning are the equivalent of Rowe's procedures and techniques that create hitherto unimagined forms in metal. By structuralist methods, language – and applied arts objects – are analysed in their fundamentals and better understood. They also illuminate their context – in Rowe's case, the applied arts in general – and alter our perception of it as a result.

The third paradigm important for an insight into Rowe's oeuvre relates to morphology, the growth of form explained in biological terms. D'Arcy Wentworth Thompson (1860–1948), an early authority on growth and form, explains the formation of, for example, clouds, hills and waves through mathematics and physics. Weights and measures, number, gravity and geometry lie at the root of form in nature, he argues, something zoologists disallow: they 'won't explain by geometry or mechanics the things which have their part in the mystery of life'.[8]

In a related discourse, the scientist Rupert Sheldrake (b.1942) questions the origin of morphic fields, new patterns that organise the universe, which come into being in the

Sometimes a big hero...

context of existing habits of nature. He suggests their formation is perhaps from 'a "higher" authority – a transcendent mind-like realm which for Pythagoras is mathematical'.[9] 'From mathematical principles, the universe [form] comes into being and evolves; by mathematical principles, everything is governed ... evolutionary creativity involves the manifestation in physical form of mathematical structures which have always existed, or rather are beyond time altogether.'[10]

These themes relate to Rowe's work, whereby mathematical principles, in the form of geometry, guide the origination of new forms, shifting existing habits in the applied arts. As we shall see, Rowe's work, drawing on these three paradigms together with phenomenological insights and Modernist ideals, caused contemporary silversmithing and the applied arts to be given renewed authority.

Rowe acknowledges that his logical search for origins of form in structural analysis is a very different strategy from 'those who choose to work more intuitively in metal', the expressionistic approach of, for example, Hiroshi Suzuki (b.1961), a Japanese former student of Rowe's. Rowe is not 'existential, looking to be free in this way. In such work the result will be different.' Yet feelings and intuition, making conscious a profound imagination, play a fundamental part in Rowe's work, albeit in a considered, intellectualised way. His mantra is derived from Kant: 'Concepts without intuitions are blind; intuitions without concepts are lame.'[11]

The realm of feelings and intuition is connected to a phenomenological viewpoint that regards all meaning in the world, even objective or scientific truth, as being grounded in human consciousness. Empirical knowledge is less important than lived experience. While structuralists seek the fundamental laws of language, so phenomenologists, more humanistically inclined, want to experience reality before theory. Reason and spirit, man and the world, are not separate but related and interdependent. Rowe seeks to embody in his containers the experience of being in the world. Inspired by the writings of, for example,

Edmund Husserl (1859–1938), Martin Heidegger (1889–1976) and Maurice Merleau-Ponty (1908–61), Rowe aims to make what he calls a 'poem-thing'. Subject and object – self and the world, content and form – are synthesised, not in an act of self-expression but of feeling and insight.

British sculptors such as Richard Deacon (b.1949) and Antony Gormley (b.1950), working through the same period as Rowe, have also been connected to phenomenological thought, meditating 'on origins and on the power of art to originate' and mediating between 'dualisms of subject and object, outside and inside, being and thinking, returning us … to the healthier totality of pre-Socratic thought'.[12]

Rowe's work relates to contemporary sculpture also in his concern to acknowledge space and time as dimensions of visual experience. Art historians Rosalind Krauss and Michael Fried have both been concerned to explore not only what constitutes an art object from the 1960s onwards, the Minimalists' preoccupation, but the experience of viewing it, the space it inhabits and the dialogue it creates with the viewer. According to Fried: 'The three-dimensionality of sculpture corresponds to the phenomenological framework in which we exist, move, perceive experience and communicate with others.'[13]

Merleau-Ponty's phenomenological approach provides 'the philosophical sanction for taking feelings seriously'[14] so that the conceptual response to art can be countered: viewers can fully appreciate the significance of feeling, gesture and bodily sensation in abstract sculpture. So also in the work of Rowe, the elision of subject and object, whereby the object spills into its surrounding space and the viewer becomes engaged in the space of the object, is a deliberate dialogue Rowe wishes to establish. Perception equates with sensation. The dynamic experience of being in the world is represented by the object's 'presence' and its form often underscores a hard-won equilibrium, 'caught', as Rowe describes it, in a 'frozen moment'. Frequently, too, what is there is underscored by what is not there – by 'absence' – another key attribute of Rowe's work.[15]

Krauss too discusses the experience of viewing the object, the space around it and the situation it creates. The dynamic experience she describes is in contrast to critic Clement Greenberg (1905–94): the sculpture is not one transcendental structure but 'the infinite sum of an indefinite series of perspectival views in each of which the object is given but in none of which it is given exhaustively'.[16] This underlines the significance Rowe attaches to the attributes of 'simultaneity' and 'relatedness' in his own work.

In capturing feeling and motion based on the experience of being in the world, a symbiosis of the physical and the mental, Rowe acknowledges the influence of cinema in his work. Cinema's simultaneity, its illusion of reality, the importance of surface and of space, layered narratives and editing techniques allow for insights into reality in which he takes delight. His play with the visual effects of gravity is a characteristic approach. He is fixing reality, achieving a kind of stasis, but of a kind that is 'charged, curiously animated'. Rowe's interest in Deconstruction, a philosophical and creative movement at its height in the 1980s, also drew on the 'dysjunction, match and mis-match' of cinema,[17] for example the films of the Soviet avant-garde film-maker Lev Kuleshov (1899–1970), whose non-sequential cutting technique inspired architects Bernard Tschumi (b.1946) and Eisenman and philosopher Jacques Derrida (b.1930).

The conjunction of feeling and thought in Rowe's oeuvre shows that geometry is used not for its own sake; it is to do with the beauty of creating new forms. The realisation of beauty is a continuous purpose in Rowe's work. It is feelings and intuitions that guide Rowe in his search for 'rightness', 'that wanting to surprise oneself with objects that make sense on several levels – one of these is sheer beauty, which seems to correspond to feelings.'

This search for rightness – 'the fascination of creating new forms and, ultimately, the beauty of that' – could suggest an essentialist distillation: a conjunction of Modernist and Japanese thinking around the ideal of pure form pared away to all but essential inherent qualities.[18] Yet Rowe does not regard this formal achievement as absolute in the way that British potter

Bernard Leach (1887-1979), say, regarded pots of the Song dynasty – in Leach's view the exemplar of an 'absolute standard'.[19] Importantly for Rowe, he and his work represent an equivocal moment, recognising that all works of art are not only born of their time but then exist in a constant state of flux across time, cultures, spaces: 'I can't believe in absolutes. I don't think anything is final. I have to remind myself that everything is strictly relative, one can say that something may be extraordinary of its kind. I know, as someone who makes things, what an infinity of choices there really is.'

Despite no fixed points, Rowe's vocabulary of forms does have an iconic base: 'My education at High Wycombe was very much based on the Bauhaus model and my subsequent thinking hasn't rejected that. I found it sympathetic. It is a basic vocabulary on which to build – the gift of the early Modernists.' For Rowe, this phrase encompasses several key movements in art and architecture of the early twentieth century. It is true that the geometry of the Bauhaus – circle, triangle, square – underpins his formal syntax, but the grammar is elaborated also by Constructivism, Cubism and Surrealism.

In a confrontation with the problem of representation in modern art – the truthful depiction of the real world and natural appearance – Cubism offered a solution. The subject of a created work would itself suggest a 'scaffolding of vertical, horizontal and diagonal lines' from which facets and planes could be hung to offer a series of related viewpoints 'fused into a single, simultaneous image'.[20] The systematic and simultaneous interaction between space, form, colour and surface decoration in a work offered a new way of apprehending lived experience. The new approach to space and form was nevertheless, as the poet Apollinaire wrote, 'impregnated with humanity'.[21]

Rowe's eloquent series of boxes begun in 1977 thrillingly applies this approach to objects in metal, the title of his groundbreaking first solo exhibition in 1978.[22] The varied viewpoints of each box and sophisticated integration of volume, line and plane yield a masterly disquisition on the perception of reality and the relationship of viewer to object and its space.

While Braque and Picasso's Cubist project gave Rowe the inspiration to explore the implications of abstraction, Constructivists and Suprematists such as Lissitsky (1890–1947), Tatlin (1885–1953) and Malevich (1878–1935) reinforced Rowe's passion for a way of thinking. While these early twentieth-century Russian artists were intent on the socialisation of art, aiming to 'organise and systematise the feelings of the revolutionary proletariat',[23] Rowe's project is to revolutionise the conception of applied art and more particularly of silversmithing in our time. By harnessing their approach – a rigorous rejection of superficial ornament and emphasis on the construction of form, more in the manner of the mechanical engineer or architect – Rowe emphasises the fusion of technology and artistic consciousness, corresponding to Malevich's aesthetic position 'in which the construction of an object would point to an immediate legible geometry'.[24]

This is not the self-expression of the American Abstract Expressionists rooted in subjectivity and emotionalism. Like Mondrian (1872–1944), who thought of his compositions in his mind before painting, Rowe proceeds logically. And yet there is a dualism in Rowe's work as there is in modern art. The rational is balanced by the acknowledgement of the unconscious imagination. Abstraction can embody feeling and desire. Hence Rowe also draws continually on the inspiration of the Surrealists whose manifesto advocated 'pure psychic automatism'.[25] Their aim was to encourage the exploration and expression of desire and the workings of the mind in an unmediated state (somewhat misappropriating Freud's aim, which was to apply psychoanalysis simply to contain and interpret, not unleash, dreams and desire). The 'true functioning of thought'[26] which the founder André Breton (1896–1966) sought to achieve is something Rowe seeks to elucidate in his works in metal; the enigmatic allusiveness, in terms of space and meaning, of de Chirico's (1888–1978) paintings remains an inspiration.

The Modern mindset thus provides Rowe with considerable freedom of approach. Postmodernism he regards as 'a logical progression' rather than an oppositional break to Modernist thought. This finds echoes in his own work in reverse: for example, his objects in the early 1970s offer an overt narrative and mannerist minituarisation by comparison with minimal works (self-reflexive and on a 1:1 scale) of the late 1970s, followed by a synthesis, a kind of late Modernism, in the *Conditions for Ornament* series of the 1980s and 1990s, and now the ongoing ellipse works begun in the late 1990s.

In this series, entitled *After Euclid*, Rowe shows a continuing engagement with the relation of objects to architectural space. In particular the *Cornerwork* pieces challenge conventional perceptions of silver. Here, silver vases and candleholders invade, and are themselves invaded by, the physical presence of walls and corners of architecture. In such apparent transgressions Rowe paradoxically tests our attitudes towards preciousness in silver objects: some pieces are literally cut in two by a corner. In a wider sense these works remind us of shared commonalities in human facture, the focus on geometric orthogonals redolent of the essential vertical and horizontal conditions of lived space.

It is important to emphasise the discourse on function in Rowe's work, since its interpretation is a key definition and preoccupation of the applied arts. Rowe's achievement in the applied arts has often been weighed purely in the direction of the metaphorical, as if utility has not been a concern. Kant's seminal observation on the nature of art – *Zweckmassigkeit ohne Zweck* (purposefulness without purpose), which has been so important to the perception of what is art or craft – has been connected to Rowe's oeuvre. This is to disregard the powerful roots in silversmithing history and the exceptionally careful and witty problem solving of form and function explored in his work.

In some works the allusion to function is clearly more conceptually significant than an actual function, but, Rowe avers: 'When I think the work has a potential for function I will follow it through. For example, the silver jugs; it is important that they are functional.' Rowe orchestrates his intentions with care. In his work the sequence of ideas can be subtly adjusted: 'Each piece is a specific discussion thing in itself. I can make a series; I can move the ideas around. If I were involved in design that was more market driven the result would be different. I think there is a place for this other kind of object.'

6 **Conditions for Ornament
   No.29, Conical Vase** 1997
   Brass, gold leaf finish
   43 x 26 x 26 cm;
   17 x 10.25 x 10.25 in
   Collection: Purchased by the
   Contemporary Art Society Special
   Collection Scheme for Birmingham
   Museums and Art Gallery
   Photograph: David Cripps

24

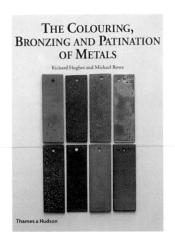

7 Cover, *The Colouring,
Bronzing and Patination
of Metals*
by Richard Hughes
and Michael Rowe
The Crafts Council, 1982 and
Thames & Hudson, 1991

Rowe's choice of metals and treatment of their surfaces signal their differing interpretation of function. He acknowledges that perhaps his most esoteric series came after the boxes and bowls of the late 1970s and early 1980s. The first series of cylinder pieces towards the mid-1980s explored the morphological aspects of vessels, eschewing actual function in favour of a commentary on possible shapes. The distinctive green patination indicated and enhanced this. Ironically, it was precisely this green patination Rowe so enigmatically re-enfranchised in silversmithing – giving non-precious metals a new lease of life – that was taken up around the world as a stylistic trope in product design and architecture throughout the 1980s.[27]

It was in the subsequent series, *Conditions for Ornament*, that ideas about utility were foregrounded. Rowe started using tin, with its deliberately vernacular associations both with kitchen and with trade – buckets and cans as well as ducting and sheeting. (There is a correspondence here with the sculpture of Richard Wentworth (b.1947), whose witty take on the everyday Rowe enjoys.) An economy of form was important. Nevertheless, alongside tinned works, he produced memorable works in gold leaf whose 'splendour and richness clearly told you to keep a respectful distance!'

So Rowe asserts that his work signals utility as well as luxury, an engagement with the everyday as well as the sublime. 'It can be very theoretical, but on another level straight-forwardly useful.' There is a democratic shift in consumption here too, with a move to offering limited editions. Rowe's work has never been widely available to buy, but its presence in museum collections and periodicals and books around the world, its significance acknowledged by peers in architecture, fine art and design attests to its enigmatic resonance. Rowe's 'project' remains consistent and all-consuming, together with his teaching and research.

For Rowe, teaching is 'a very important part of what I do. I see the role of a teacher as someone who helps another to help themselves. It is a constant challenge.' This process is continually tested and enhanced by Rowe's teaching and travelling round the world, often in the company of his long-term partner Iene Ambar, the Chinese artist born in Indonesia. Simone ten Hompel (b.1960), a prominent former student of Rowe's at the Royal College of Art, where he has taught for 20 years, echoes the widespread appreciation of his approach: 'I'm not sure teacher is a good description. He is more a partner, someone who discussed things with me. He didn't really show me things; it was there for me to find. We didn't talk about techniques, but content. In the field of metalwork and silversmithing, Michael is like a key: his theorising took the practice out of the field into other realms of discussion and afterwards got reintroduced back into the field – like a metamorphosis. So he opened the boundaries of our field.'

Perhaps a reason for the power of Rowe's objects in metal and their responsive audience lies in his ability to realise in single tangible entities transcendent poetic beauty and complexities of thought. He reconciles the dualities evident in human experience, revealed through the points of reference he has chosen to inform his project: structuralism versus phenomenology, Cubism/Constructivism versus Surrealism, the apparent spontaneity of morphology tempered by the understanding that rules of geometry underlie form generation.

Rowe speaks fervently of the creative cycle whereby 'self-analysis of the fundamentals has gradually spread through all the arts'. He believes the deconstructive process has underpinned all visual cultural practice in the twentieth century and discusses how Greenberg sought to analyse and insist on the fundamentals of painting as a result of the threat from photography.[28] Significantly Rowe says: 'It's the way the rebuilding takes place that fascinates me, which for some reason hasn't happened in metal. Indeed the applied arts in general have avoided it, treating the structural discoveries of painting, sculpture and architecture merely as an image bank, providing ready made "visual givens" that have fuelled the creation of styles.'

Herein lies Rowe's achievement and his role in both silversmithing and in the applied arts as a whole since the 1970s, wherein analysis and rebuilding have been his aim. As a student at the Royal College of Art at the end of the 1960s, Rowe questioned the assumption that to be successful one had to work as a consultant designer to manufacturers. He believed that a more effective mode of working for realising the flow of ideas was to set up autonomously in a studio environment, 'a laboratory of forms and ideas'.

A number of peers, especially in ceramics, shared this aim, extending the philosophy and practice of William Morris (1834–96) and of Bernard Leach. In eastern Europe and in Scandinavia, a more orthodox link between craftsman and industry prevailed. But in the United States and Britain in the 1970s, and gradually throughout Europe, then Australia and Japan, there grew a widespread emphasis on the role of the individual maker in the production of things. In metalwork, important practitioners have developed the practice, and one can cite, for example Sigurd Persson (b.1914, Sweden), Helen Shirk (b.1942, USA), Werner Bunck (b.1943, Germany) and Lino Sabattini (b.1925, Italy).

This development was especially encouraged in Britain where a government-funded advisory committee (now the Crafts Council) was established in 1971, with its influential exhibitions programme and magazine growing out of the important exhibition *The Craftsman's Art* at the Victoria and Albert Museum in 1973. Rowe played a central part in this 'crafts revival',[29] one of the few craftspeople consciously forging an avant-garde in the crafts, participating in the V&A exhibition, featuring in the first issue of *Crafts* magazine, having a solo exhibition in the Crafts Council gallery and having his work acquired for the Council's national collection of crafts all within five years.

Over the past 30 years, the applied arts have gathered momentum worldwide, with the growth of funded organisations, exhibitions with catalogues in public and private galleries, new periodicals, educational expansion, research, a growth in museum collecting of the contemporary, in public and private commissions and in activity in the auction rooms.

8 Michael Rowe receiving
The Golden Ring of Honour
from the Gesellschaft
für Goldschmiedekunst,
Schloss Philippsruhe,
Hanau, Germany 2002
from left to right:
Yasuki Hiramatsu
Peter Chang
Barbara Santos-Shaw
Mrs Yasuki Hiramatsu
Helen Drutt-English
Hermann Jünger
Peter Skubic
Michael Rowe
Beatriz Chadour-Sampson
Iene Ambar (partially hidden)
Giampaolo Babetto
Raymond Sampson
Photographer: Ichiro Furuichi

An international network of applied arts activity among practitioners and advocates has developed and in all these areas Rowe has played a central role, as maker, teacher and researcher. In demand throughout the world, Rowe has received the most prestigious accolades, including the first Decorative Art Award from Sotheby's in 1988, a Japan Foundation Artist's Fellowship in 1993, and above all, in 2002, The Golden Ring of Honour from the Gesellschaft für Goldschmiedekunst in Germany. Rowe is the first Briton to receive this award, widely regarded as the highest honour in the world of gold and silversmithing.

The reasons for such approbation are compelling: in choosing to work 'on the outer limits of function' (the potter Alison Britton's memorable phrase in 1982[30]) Rowe established silversmithing as an arena for avant-garde thought. Inspired by Christopher Dresser (1834–1904) in the nineteenth century and the Viennese Josef Hoffman (1870–1956) and the Bauhaus silversmiths such as Marianne Brandt (1893–1983) in the early twentieth century, whose works marked a new path in their time, Rowe believed that handmade objects in his own time could be both abstract and carriers of thought and meaning that would resonate with contemporary experience and connect with the wider cultural discourse.

The essential commitment to the discipline of silversmithing gave authority and singularity to his quest. His fastidious deployment of the techniques and processes of silversmithing has been enhanced by the acuity of choice of material for each object. His research, with colleague Richard Hughes, into the colouring, bronzing and patination of metals gave him and the world new opportunities for the expression of ideas and materiality in metals of all kinds.[31] He is respected internationally as a teacher whose students have learned from him how to think for themselves, to interrogate their material and their intention. Rowe has reappraised the role and meaning of the decorative arts and the domestic object, initiated in a long trajectory from the Renaissance, through the Enlightenment, the Industrial Revolution, the Arts and Crafts movement and the Bauhaus, and expanded the possibilities for metalwork in visual culture.

9 **After Euclid:**
Cornerwork 2003
925 silver
14.5 x 20.5 x 14 cm; 5.75 x 8 x 5.5 in
Private collection
Photograph: Michael Harvey

Notes

1 The 'project' is Rowe's description of his oeuvre. All Rowe's quoted remarks are from conversations with the author that took place between June and October 2002.

2 See for example Gaston Bachelard, *The Right To Dream (Le Droit de Rever)*, French translation by J. A. Underwood, Dallas Institute Press, Dallas, 1988.

3 Christopher Alexander, *Notes on the Synthesis of Form*, Harvard University Press, 1964.

4 Adolf Loos, 'Ornament and Crime', essay of 1908 reprinted in *The Architecture of Adolf Loos*, Arts Council, London, 1985.

5 Kenneth Frampton, *Modern Architecture: A Critical History,* third edition, Thames and Hudson, London, 1992.

6 Ferdinand de Saussure, *Course de Linguistique Générale,* translated edition edited by Charles Bally and Albert Sechehaye, Fonatana, London, 1974.

7 Quoted in Richard Kearney, *Modern Movements in European Philosophy: Phenomenology, Critical Theory, Structuralism,* second edition, Manchester University Press, Manchester, 1994.

8 D'Arcy Wentworth Thompson, *On Growth and Form*, first published 1917, this edition Cambridge University Press, 1969.

9 Rupert Sheldrake, *The Rebirth of Nature: the Greening of Science and God,* Century, London, 1990

10 Ibid.

11 Ernst Mach's rephrasing of Immanuel Kant (in *Kritik der Reinen Vernunft* 1787) in his book *Space and Geometry*, Paul Kegan, Trubner, Trench, London, 1906.

12 Stuart Morgan essay in *Transformations: New Sculpture from Britain*, British Council, London, 1983.

13 Michael Fried, *Art and Objecthood: Essays and Reviews*, Univsersity of Chicago Press, Chicago, 1998.

14 Alex Potts, *The Sculptural Imagination: Figurative, Modernist, Minimalist,* Yale University Press, New Haven and London, 2000.

15 All quoted words from Michael Rowe.

16 Rosalind Krauss, *Passages in Modern Sculpture*, MIT Press, Massachusetts, 1981 (paperback edition).

17 Kenneth Frampton, op.cit.

18 See Soetsu Yanagi, *The Unknown Craftsman: A Japanese Insight into Beauty,* Kodansha International, Tokyo, 1972.

19 See Bernard Leach, 'Towards a standard', chapter 1 of *A Potter's Book*, Faber and Faber, London, 1940.

20 John Golding, essay on 'Cubism' in Nikos Stangos (ed.) *Concepts of Modern Art*, Thames and Hudson, London, 1985.

21 Guillaume Apollinaire, *Les Peintres Cubistes*, Paris, 1913, quoted by John Golding, ibid.

22 *Objects in Metal*, Crafts Advisory Committee, London, 1978.

23 Aaaron Scharf, 'Constructivism', in Nikos Stangos (ed.), op.cit.

24 Suzi Gablik, essay on 'Minimalism', ibid.

25 André Breton, *Manifestoes of Surrealism*, Paris 1962, referred to in Dawn Ades, essay on 'Dada and Surrealism', ibid.

26 Quoted by Dawn Ades, ibid.

27 Full discussion of this in 'Metalwork and Metamorphosis', an essay by Martina Margetts in *The Chemistry Set*, Crafts Council, London, 1993.

28 John O'Brien (ed.) Clement Greenberg: *The Collected Essays and Criticism, Volume 4: Modernism with a Vengeance 1959-1969,* University of Chicago Press, Chicago, 1993.

29 See Martina Margetts, *Contemporary British Crafts*, British Council, London, 1988 and *Objects of Our Time,* Crafts Council, London, 1996; also Tanya Harrod, *The Crafts in Britain in the 20th Century*, Yale University Press, New Haven and London, 1999.

30 Alison Britton essay in *The Maker's Eye*, Crafts Council, London, 1981; see also Martina Margetts, *Beyond Material: the New Crafts of the 90s*, Oriel Mostyn Gallery, Llandudno, 1998.

31 Richard Hughes and Michael Rowe, *The Colouring, Bronzing and Patination of Metals*, Crafts Council, 1982, reprinted Thames and Hudson, London, 1991.

30

Plate XL

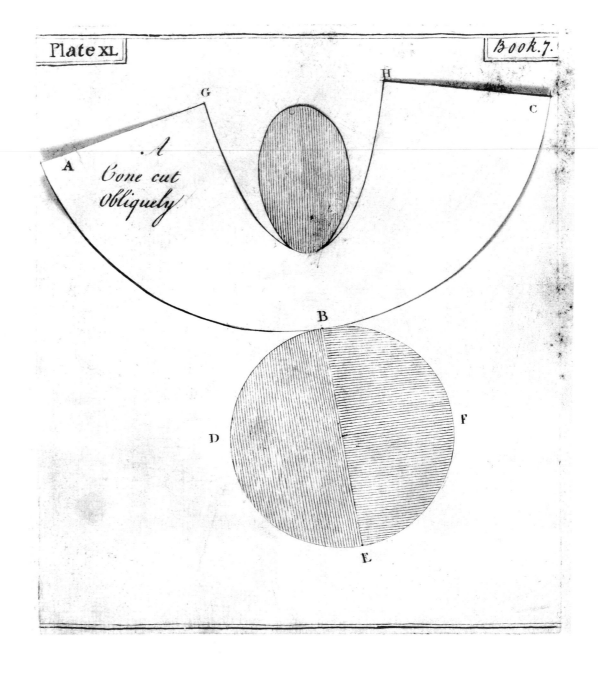

Book. 7

A
Cone cut
Obliquely

A cone cut obliquely
Richard Hill

10 A Cone Cut Obliquely
Plate XL from John Lodge Cowley,
An Appendix to Euclid's Elements,
London 1758

Take a rectangular piece of paper, curve it round, join the two edges together and you have a cylinder. Making a cone needs more planning: cut out a disk, take a slice out of it then bend it round. To make a bucket shape – a cone with the point cut off – you must cut out a gently curved strip, like a collar, and then bend it round. Can you make a hemispherical bowl out of a piece of paper? Of course not. The surface of a cone or a cylinder is curved only once but a hemispherical bowl is doubly curved and it is simply a fact about paper that it will only bend or fold in one direction at a time (although its performance changes if you wet it). You can, on the other hand, make a bowl out of metal, not by bending and folding but by 'raising' or 'sinking'. These delightful terms denote the laborious work of hammering the sheet, each blow making a small depression and pushing a ripple of metal outwards. Metal is like very recalcitrant pastry or clay; you can mould it but only with hammers or presses and not just with your fingers. The expressive possibilities of this hammering-moulding are astonishing, as the picture of the cup by Dutch silversmith Adam van Vianen (1565–1627) shows (12). The possibilities offered by folding and bending are no less astonishing but they tend towards more austere and measured kinds of beauty as seen in the Mycenaen Cup (11). Michael Rowe's work, justly celebrated in this volume and in the exhibition that it accompanies, shows us just how various these beauties can be.

For most of his career Rowe has worked within the disciplines of cutting, bending and folding sheet metal. Even his series of luscious bowls – for example *Bowl* (1980) (3) – which naturally have doubly curved surfaces, were made by 'spinning' silver sheet on a lathe rather than by hammering it into its final form. Spinning is a more geometrical operation than hammering: one can rotate a two-dimensional curve diagrammatically, but spinning does this for real. Evidently Rowe's preference for geometrically disciplined techniques of metalwork is deeply rooted, but out of it has come great aesthetic richness.

Consider paper as the interface, the connecting medium, between geometry and Rowe's metalworking procedures. Complex objects can be depicted on paper. Some skill and care would be needed to draw the van Vianen cup but its complex outline and the surface relief

11 **Cup from Citadel of Mycenae, Tomb IV, known as the Cup of Nestor**
Gold, folded, pierced and chased sheet
Second half of the sixteenth century BC
14.5 cm
Collection: National Museum, Athens

could be captured in line and shading. There is however a category of objects that can be drawn on paper and then made out of the paper itself. 'A cone cut obliquely' is the title of one of the plates in John Lodge Cowley's *Appendix to Euclid's Elements*, published in 1758 (10). It is a beautiful image, bringing together the stolid circle, the flighty collar shape and the sensuous bead of the ellipse. In fact the shapes are cut round so that the reader can fold the parts together and make the cone, with its oblique cut, rise up from the page. Cowley's aim was to make geometry more understandable by making geometrical figures real, tactile, foldable, because, as he put it, '... 'tis no easy matter to form distinct and just ideas concerning bodies and their sections, when represented only according to their perspective appearance ...'.

Objects that can be both drawn on paper and made out of paper, such as Cowley's fold-up diagrams, can be described as having 'ruled' and 'developable' surfaces. A ruled surface is one that can be made out of straight lines: imagine putting a ruler against the face of a cone or cylinder and moving it around the surface so that it stays in contact. A developable surface is one where the lines that make up the surface can also be made to lie flat, keeping their lengths and the distances between them intact. Again, cones and cylinders are simple examples, but such surfaces can be very complex and would include a starched and crimped ruff or the rippling shapes of Alvar Aalto's (1898–1976) glassware. It is important to remember that not all ruled surfaces are developable. A good example is the 'hyperbolic paraboloid', the source of a variety of cunning concrete roof structures where a double curved surface is cast on straight lengths of shuttering, each slightly skew in relation to its neighbours.

A developable surface can be drawn and the drawing can then be folded or bent to make the surface itself. You then have a physical model of your object. If you want to make it in sheet metal, an accurate drawing on paper or card can serve as a template and, as Michael Rowe does, you can prick through the template with a sharp point to define the shape of the metal, then proceed to cut, bend and join. One could say that objects with developable

Adam van Vianen
(1565–1627)
12 **Standing Cup and Cover**
1614
Silver gilt, raised, cast and chased
25.5 cm
© Rijksmuseum, Amsterdam

surfaces are amphibious and can survive in either two or three dimensions. There is a continuity with Rowe's earlier interests in ambiguous perspective effects created by the play of three-dimensional objects against a two-dimensional field of vision, as in *Condiment Centrepiece* (1976) (27) or *Copper Box* (1977) (32).

Rowe has further extended the repertoire of 'developable surfaces' in order to arrive at the distinctive form-world of the objects that he has produced since about 1984. The first point to note is his concentration on the potential of the cone and the cylinder for the dominant form of a design. This is partly because of their geometrical simplicity but mainly because they form the basis of most kinds of jugs, cups, bottles, jars and so on. They have a foot in elementary geometry and a foot in practical life: they are children of the humble bucket family as well as heirs of the pure forms of ancient geometry. In fact it is the individuality or specificity of Rowe's forms, the sense that they live in our world rather than a cosmic space, that makes them compelling. The sources of their individuality, and thus of the formal compositional aspects of Rowe's work, are complex. However, they belong in a long tradition of formal invention in which geometrical objects are considered as having an inner life, a tradition in which the artist's role is to expose this life to view. The neo-classical architect Karl Friedrich Schinkel (1781–1841) – whose masterpiece is the Altes Museum in Berlin, designed in 1822–3 – expressed this in a memorable way:[1]

> *Striving, budding, crystallizing, unfolding, driving, a splitting, fitting, drifting,*
> *floating, pulling, pressing, bending, bearing, placing, vibrating, connecting, holding,*
> *a lying and resting – where the latter, which contrasts with the kinetic properties,*
> *must be an intentional and obvious repose, and therefore also a living action – these*
> *are the ways in which architecture must manifest life.*

The composition of many of Rowe's pieces – for example *Conditions for Ornament No.14* (1992) (78), *Conical Vessel* (1992) (80) or *Conditions for Ornament No.29* (1997) (6) – can be understood as the result of such inner forces.

This type of formal invention runs parallel to an expansion of the repertoire of forms in another respect. This occurs in the way that the dominant forms are articulated or the way that smaller forms cluster around them. Consider first the use of faceted surfaces, for example in *Cylindrical Vessel* (1984) (52), which vividly demonstrates their interchangeability with curved surfaces in the form of a larger object. Faceted surfaces are just as developable as curved ones, although in practice Rowe prefers to make them out of joined strips rather than folded sheet in order to keep the facet edges crisp. This joining method is essential in another variety of subsidiary object, namely the 'pods' or 'buds' that can be seen attached to *Conditions for Ornament Nos.6 and 12* (1988 and 1990) (5 and 74). They are made from flat sheet, cut into pointed segments then curved and joined to make a composite object. They are the kind of reconciliation of flat and curved that lies behind map projections in which a curved world is presented on a flat sheet; or that forms the back of a lute, necessarily made out of flat strips of wood curved in only one direction but joined to make a gently faceted surface.

Now consider a jug as a practical object. It has a handle, a lip and, in the act of pouring, a column of liquid joining it to the receiving container or dish. One of Rowe's aims has been to give expression to these useful aspects of vessels, again subtly extending the formal repertoire, adding subsidiary elements to the main bodies of the vessels themselves. An abstracted kind of pouring can be made out of developable surfaces combined into little sets of pipes as in *Lidded Container* (in brass and gold leaf, 1985) (60), or made into flowing sheets as in the lovely *Conditions for Ornament No.5* (1988) (69). The buds, by virtue of their organic associations, take on the task of representing the life that inhabits an abstract form when it works as a vessel.

Rowe's form-world is wide enough to embrace ranges of emotional tone. Some have a forbidding aspect, such as *Conditions for Ornament No.16* (1992) (81), some are grand and dignified such as *Conditions for Ornament No.28* (1996) (99) and some have a comic air. For example *Conditions for Ornament No.2* (1988) (67) is a demonstration of the properties of cylinders and cones but it is also a line-up of characters, one standing smartly to attention, another with carelessly drooped shoulders.

Someone might say that there is more of the exuberance of van Vianen than of the geometrical discipline of sheet metalwork in the forms that surround us today: plastic moulding now makes a free-form sculpted shape as easy to manufacture as a cylinder. The washing-up liquid bottle or the casing of a scanner can take on any curvaceous shape that moulding will allow. It is true that sheet metalwork is still essential in some fields, and air-conditioning ductwork, for example, has exactly the charm of not-quite-pure geometry as do Rowe's objects. But as an evocation of a domestic world of containers Rowe's form-world is austere and looks back to an earlier age of production. Tanya Harrod has noted a paradox in Modernist writing on the arts and crafts in the early twentieth century, namely 'that an important part of being modern was to be anti-modern'.[2] There is no doubt about the modernity of Rowe's work, and in particular its affinity with the abstract and minimalist traditions of Modernism. However there is also an anti-modernity, an attachment to artisanal production methods in preference to the ability of modern techniques to press or mould any shape and any elaboration that one might wish. The issue that Harrod is alluding to – whether Le Corbusier (1887–1965), whom she cites, is in mind, or perhaps Adolf Loos (1870–1933) or William Morris (1834–96) – is an attachment to methods of production the rules of which strictly determine a limited set of typical forms. Techniques that can make just anything, or imitate just anything, are treated with some reserve. As we can see, sheet metalwork provides Rowe with a kind of defence against this unravelling of formal rules.

The architectural critic and historian Kenneth Frampton has argued that a struggle for the 'tectonic' character of architecture – for its outward forms to have a disciplined relation to the necessities of construction – was a key feature of twentieth-century Modernism. In his view it forms a focus of resistance to the tendency for all things to be changeable one into another, a rebuke to the tendency towards 'the reduction of the entire world to one vast commodity'.[3] The 'tectonic' outlook has the two-edged character that Harrod describes, asserting modernity and returning to sources, radical and conservative at once.

This two-edged aspect of Modernism can be found in Rowe's work. However it is at a tangent to the views he has expressed in his own writings. As well as being a meticulous craftsman, Rowe is a voracious and careful reader of cultural and philosophical theory. He has referred to the arguments made in the 1970s by the architect and writer Peter Eisenman (b.1932) about the nature of Modernism.[4] Eisenman's view was that Modernism placed on the artist a responsibility to question and subvert the normal assumptions of a given art form. The conventional view is that architecture and the other applied arts have as their basis the satisfying of function: this is what makes them distinctive in the larger system of the arts. Eisenman argued that the responsibility of the modern designer or architect is therefore to criticise just that assumption, and to make the criticism thematic to their work. Thus, with considerable aplomb, Eisenman proceeded to design a house that was deliberately difficult to live in, in defiance of what he considered to be a falsely Modernist attachment to ease, comfort and social purpose.

This 'deconstructionist' strand of Modernist theory contributed to Rowe's own subversion of the usefulness of containers and vessels. The techniques included giving the objects flanged base plates that fixed them in position on the edge of a surface. A key useful feature of a vase – that one may put it where one pleases – was thereby subverted. A highly original and alluring series of objects resulted, for example *Conditions for Ornament Nos.4, 6 and 7* (1988) (72, 5 and 70). Tethering the vessel form to flat plates has the effect of restricting their position but it simultaneously fixes them to continuous horizontal and vertical planes. It is as if a diagram from 'descriptive geometry' – in which space is represented as three intersecting flat planes – has been made real. The object is restricted in position by the sheet metal plates, but their existence alludes to a continuous and universal space: the object is, as it were, trapped *here*, but the *here* could be anywhere.

I doubt however that usefulness has really been subverted. More likely it has been displaced and carries on its work elsewhere. In fact Eisenman's interest in a deconstructionist view of Modernism was quite short-lived and has been replaced by a more relaxed view which

allows merely that usefulness can be satisfied in a great variety of formal settings. Rowe
continues to explore the possibilities of a subversive view of the form/function issue, but he
has also pointed out that the objects in question are not entirely useless. They are still made
as leak-proof containers and could, for example, act as flower vases. The conclusion that we
should draw is that usefulness or 'function' is an essentially empirical matter, and while it is
open to practical modification or displacement its conceptual character is highly elusive and
largely resistant to change or subversion by argument. In the event a consequence of Rowe's
interest in the deconstructionist agenda has been to further extend his formal repertoire. For
example the flat sheets that tethered objects to corners or edges of surfaces could also be
used in counterpoint to the faceted buds that make veiled reference to the usefulness of
vessels, as in *Conditions for Ornament No.11* (1989) (73).

Usefulness may lose most of its practical purchase but it lingers in allusive forms. Consider,
in addition to the representations of flowing liquid, spouts, lips and handles, its contribution
to the compositional energy of many of the objects. Small vessels – jugs, bowls and cups –
have to be moved in order to be useful. Rowe represents these practical movements, or
perhaps the record of completed movements, in numerous ways. Note for example the
suggestion of cascading movement in *Conditions for Ornament Nos.15 and 25* (1992 and
1994) (79 and 95); the sense of liquid being measured out in *Conical Vessel* (1993) (84);
the full and the empty vessel side by side in *Conditions for Ornament No.18* (1993) (85); or
the full and half-full volumes, weighty with their imagined liquids, that are attached to the
main form of the beautiful *Conditions for Ornament No.22* (1994) (90).

Let us take the usefulness issue in a slightly different direction. If you don't use an object
and have no interest in it being used by others your attitude to it will change. The object
may cease to be of any interest to you at all or your attitude may shift from a practical to
an aesthetic one. A shift in attitude towards the status of an object may also have
'institutional' consequences. A jug or a kettle belongs in a kitchen but an object with little
or highly constrained usefulness may be more at home in an art gallery. Imagine for

example that *Conditions for Ornament Nos.4, 6 or 7* (1988) (72, 5 and 70) were moved to the Tate Modern and placed near to Donald Judd's (1928-94) *Untitled* (1973) (13) and Naum Gabo's (1890-1977) *Spiral: Model for Spheric Theme* (n.d.) (14). Pieces by Rowe, Gabo and Judd would belong together by virtue of their simplicity of form, their exploitation of developable surfaces and their use of sheet materials. Then a thought might emerge concerning the arbitrariness of the institutional divisions that keep Rowe's work in the orbit of the crafts rather than that of fine art.

A counter-thought soon takes over: that such a juxtaposition of objects would actually bring out the distinctiveness of the craft tradition and the contribution it can make to the larger world of the visual arts. One would see very quickly how different Rowe's work is from that of a modern sculptor, and note that the difference comes from immersion in a craft culture in which use and production, however elliptically or obliquely expressed, are thematic to each object, endowing it with life and beauty. The whole body of work then becomes a vindication of the craft tradition and of the contribution it can make to the world of the visual arts.

Donald Judd (1928–1994)
13 **Untitled** 1973
(Tate no. T01727)
Copper relief
Collection: Tate Modern, London
© Estate of Donald Judd/VAGA,
New York/DACS, London 2002
Photographer: © Tate, London, 2003

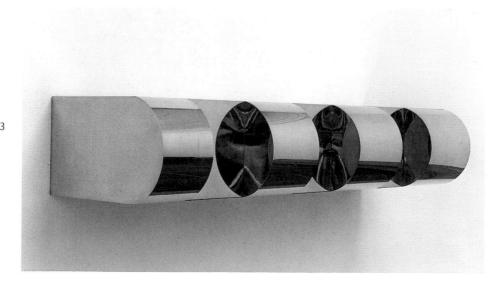

Notes

1 Quoted in Hermann G. Pundt, *Schinkel's Berlin: A Study in Environmental Planning*, Cambridge, Mass., Harvard University Press, 1972, p.195.

2 Tanya Harrod, *The Crafts in Britain in the 20th Century*, London and New Haven, Yale University Press, 1999, p.145.

3 Kenneth Frampton, *Studies in Tectonic Culture: The Poetics of Construction in Nineteenth and Twentieth Century Architecture*, Cambridge, Mass., MIT Press, 1995, p.376.

4 See for example Peter Eisenman, 'Misreading', in *House of Cards*, New York, Oxford University Press, 1975.

Naum Gabo (1890–1977)
14 **Spiral: Model for Spheric Theme** n.d.
(Tate no. T02173)
Translucent plastic
12 x 9.2 x 9.2 cm;
4.75 x 3.75 x 3.75 in
Collection: Tate Modern, London
The works of Naum Gabo
© Nina Williams
Reproduced courtesy Tate,
London, 2003

15 **Jewel Box** 1964
Brass
6.5 x 20.2 x 8.7 cm;
2.5 x 8 x 3.5 in
Private collection
Photograph: David Bailey

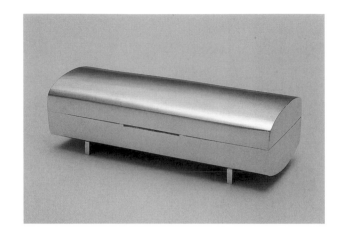

16 **Cigarette Box** 1965
Silver plated brass, acrylic
9.7 x 11.5 x 9.4 cm;
3.75 x 4.5 x 3.75 in
Private collection
Photograph: David Bailey

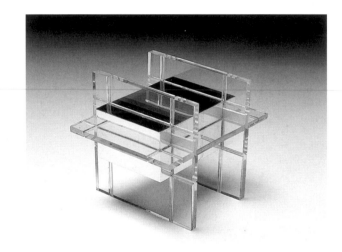

left
17 **Ring** 1965
Brass
4.5 x 4 x 4 cm;
1.75 x 1.5 x 1.5 in
Private collection
Photograph: Michael Rowe

right
18 **Sunglass Design** 1972
Polaroid Ltd
Summer Collection, 1972
Promotional photograph

19 **Double Inkwell** 1971
Bronze, black patination
9.8 x 15.8 x 16.7 cm;
3.75 x 6.25 x 6.5 in
Private collection
Photograph: David Bailey

43

20 **Double Inkwell** 1971
Bronze, green patination
11.5 x 10 x 16.8 cm;
4.5 x 4 x 6.5 in
Private collection
Photograph: Michael Rowe

21 Drinking Cup 1972
925 silver
11.3 x 10.7 x 10 cm;
4.5 x 4.25 x 4 in
Private collection
Photo: David Bailey

44

22 Desk Set 1972
925 silver
12 x 32 x 34 cm;
5.75 x 12.5 x 13.5 in
Private collection
Photograph: Michael Rowe

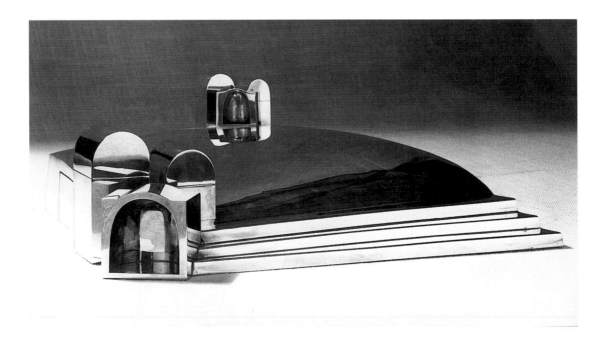

23 **Pomander** 1972
Copper, green patination,
925 silver
32 x 41.5 x 53 cm;
12.5 x 16.25 x 21 in
Private collection
Photograph: Richard Davies

24 **Double Inkwell** 1973
925 silver
18 x 25 x 17 cm;
7 x 9.75 x 6.75 in
Private collection
Photograph: Michael Rowe

25 **Pomander** 1973
925 silver
21.5 x 57 cm; 8.5 x 22.5 in
Collection: Crafts Council, London
Photograph: David Cripps

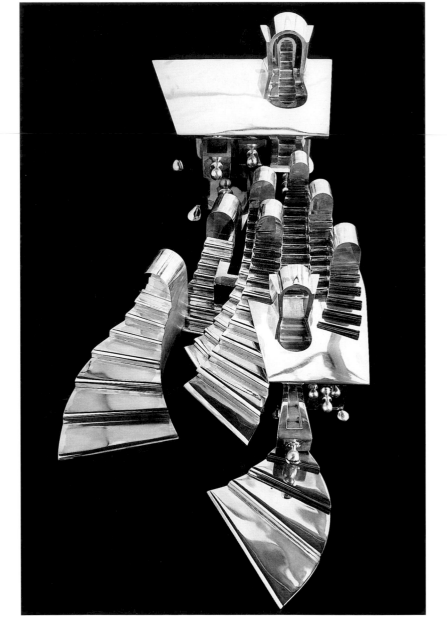

26 **Pomander** 1975
925 silver
25 x 20 x 10 cm; 9.75 x 8 x 4 in
Commissioned by Liberty & Co. Ltd.
Now lost
Photograph: David Cripps

27 **Condiment Centrepiece** 1976
925 silver
43.2 x 30.5 x 30.5 cm; 17 x 12 x 12 in
Collection: 401½ Collection
Photograph: Michael Freeman

28 **Exploratory Drawing for Box** 1977
Pencil on paper
59.4 x 42 cm; 23.5 x 16.5 in
Collection: Rowe Archive

29 **Exploratory Drawing for Box** 1977
Pencil on paper
59.4 x 42 cm; 23.5 x 16.5 in
Collection: Rowe Archive

48

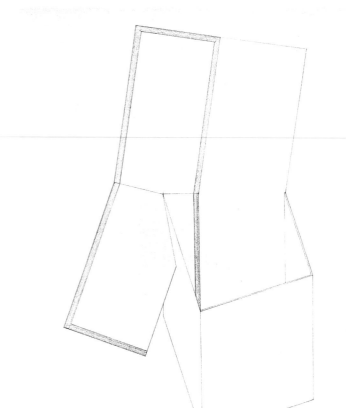

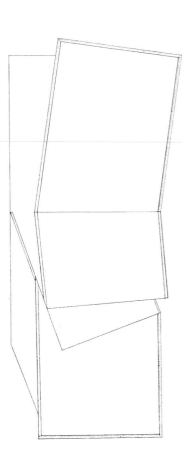

30 **Exploratory Drawing for Box** 1977
Pencil on paper
59.4 x 42 cm; 23.5 x 16.5 in
Collection: Rowe Archive

31 **Exploratory Drawing for Box** 1977
Pencil on paper
59.4 x 42 cm; 23.5 x 16.5 in
Collection: Rowe Archive

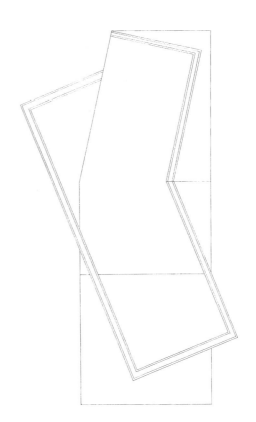

34 **Box** 1978
925 silver, copper
22.5 x 12.5 x 10 cm;
9 x 5 x 4 in
Private collection
Photograph: David Cripps

opposite
35 **Box** 1978
925 silver, copper
29 x 18 x 22.5 cm;
11.5 x 7 x 8.5 in
Collection: Crafts Council, London
Photograph: David Cripps

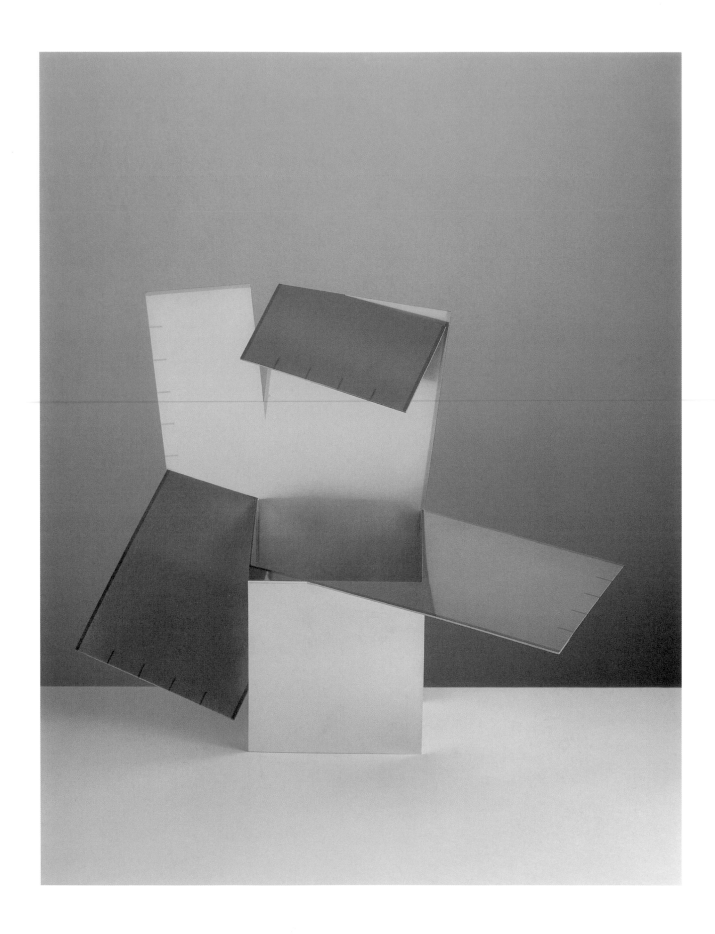

opposite

36 **Box** 1978
925 silver, 9 carat red gold,
25 x 33 x 20 cm; 9.75 x 13 x 8 in
Private collection
Photograph: David Cripps

37 **Box** 1978
Copper, 925 silver
21.75 x 15 x 9 cm; 8.5 x 6 x 3.5 in
Private collection
Photograph: David Cripps

38 **Box** 1978
Brass, brown patination
28 x 13.5 x 17 cm; 11 x 5.25 x 6.75 in
Private collection
Photograph: Ian Haigh

42 **Drawing for a Bowl** 1980
(see image 44)
Pencil and red ink on paper
59.4 x 42 cm; 23.5 x 16.5 in
Collection: Birmingham Museums
and Art Gallery
Photograph: David Bailey

43 **Drawing for a Bowl** 1979
(see image 3)
Pencil and red ink on paper
59.4 x 42 cm; 23.5 x 16.5 in
Collection: Rowe Archive
Photograph: David Bailey

opposite

44 **Bowl** 1980
925 silver, copper
8 x 40 x 26 cm; 3 x 15.75 x 10.25 in
Collection: Birmingham Museums
and Art Gallery
Photograph: Ian Haigh

45 **Bowl** 1981
Brass, brown patination
10 x 44 x 30 cm; 4 x 17.25 x 11.75 in
Collection: Leeds Museums and
Galleries (Lotherton Hall)
Photograph: Ian Haigh

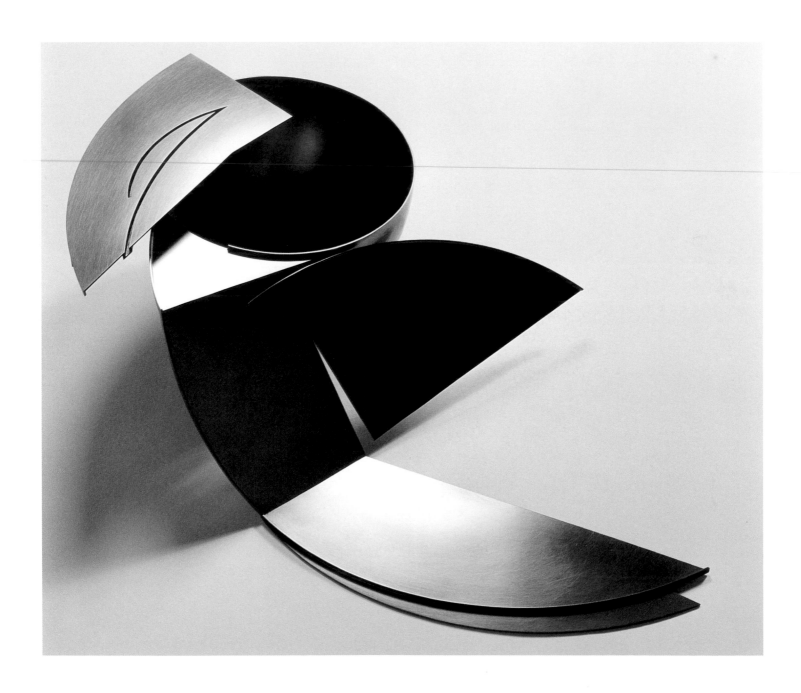

46 **Bowl** 1981
Brass, brown patination
14 x 30 x 20 cm; 5.5 x 11.75 x 8 in
Collection: Crafts Council, London
Photograph: Ian Dobbie

50 **Cylindrical Vessel** 1982
Brass, green patination
15 x 25 x 20 cm; 6 x 9.75 x 8 in
Collection: 401½ Collection
Photograph: Ian Haigh

51 **Cylindrical Vessel** 1983
Brass, gold leaf finish
20 x 20 x 15 cm; 8 x 8 x 6 in
Collection: Badisches Landesmuseum,
Karlsruhe
Photograph: Ian Haigh

52 **Cylindrical Vessel** 1984
Brass, green patination
26 x 34 x 19.5 cm; 10.25 x 13.5 x 7.75 in
Private collection
Photograph: Ian Haigh

53 **Cylindrical Vessel** 1985
Brass, green patination
34.5 x 37 x 28 cm; 13.5 x 14.5 x 11 in
Private collection
Photograph: Ian Haigh

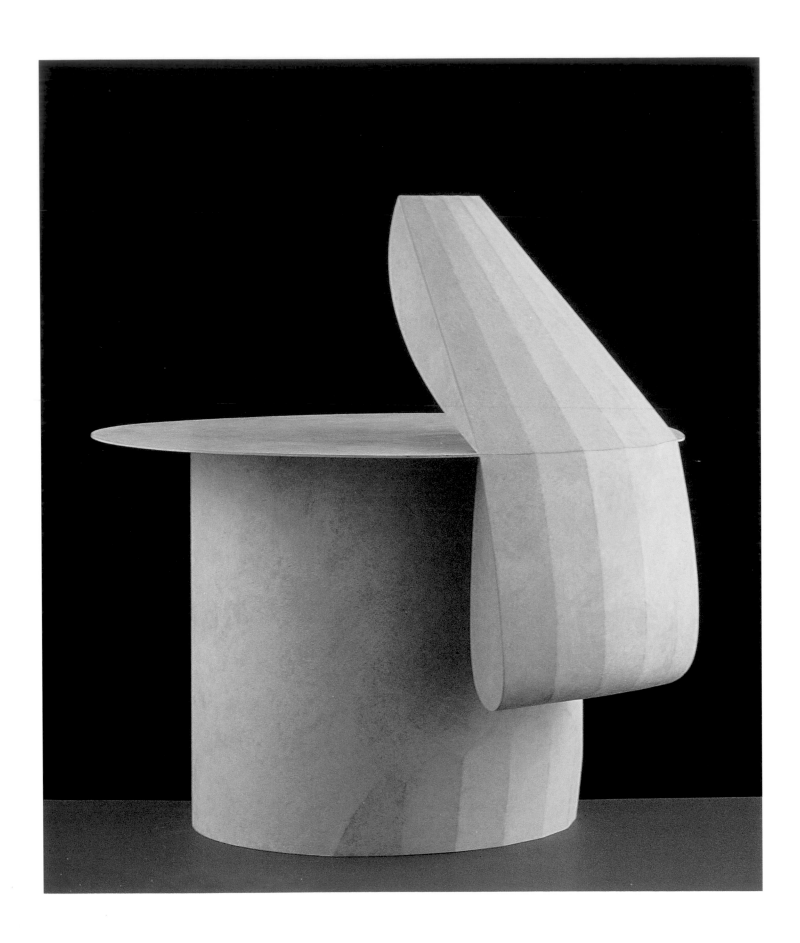

opposite

54 **Lidded Container** 1985
Brass, green patination
32 x 31.5 x 31 cm; 12.5 x 12.25 x 12 in
Collection: Crafts Council, London
Photograph: David Cripps

55 **Lidded Container** 1985
Brass, tin finish
60 x 20 x 25 cm; 23.5 x 8 x 9.75 in
Collection: Leeds Museums
and Galleries (Lotherton Hall)
Photograph: Ian Haigh

56 **Cylindrical Vessel** 1985
Brass, tin finish
24.2 x 28 x 29.5 cm; 9.5 x 11 x 11.75 in
Collection: Art Gallery of Western Australia
Photograph: Ian Haigh

61 Cylindrical Vessel 1986
Brass, tin finish
20 x 35 x 35 cm;
20 x 13.75 x 13.75 in
Private collection
Photograph: Ian Haigh

62 Cylindrical Vessel 1986
Brass, gold leaf finish
35 x 35 x 35 cm;
13.75 x 13.75 x 13.75 in
Collection: Shipley Art Gallery,
Gateshead, Tyne and Wear Museums
Photograph: Ian Haigh

opposite
63 Cylindrical Vessel 1986
Brass, tin finish
40 x 30 x 30 cm;
15.75 x 11.75 x 11.75 in
Private collection
Photograph: Ian Haigh

64 Cylindrical Vessel 1987
Bronze and steel
Made during the Gulbenkian
Foundation Vessel Workshop
10 x 16.5 x 10 cm;
4 x 6.5 x 4 in
Private collection
Photograph: Michael Harvey

65 Cylindrical Vessel 1987
Bronze and steel
Made during the Gulbenkian
Foundation Vessel Workshop
16 x 35 x 21 cm;
6.25 x 13.75 x 8.25 in
Private collection
Photograph: David Cripps

66 **Conditions for Ornament No.1,**
Cylindrical Vessel 1987
Brass, gold leaf finish
15 x 50 x 50 cm;
6 x 19.75 x 19.75 in
Collection: Miharudo Gallery, Tokyo
Photograph: Masaaki Sekiya

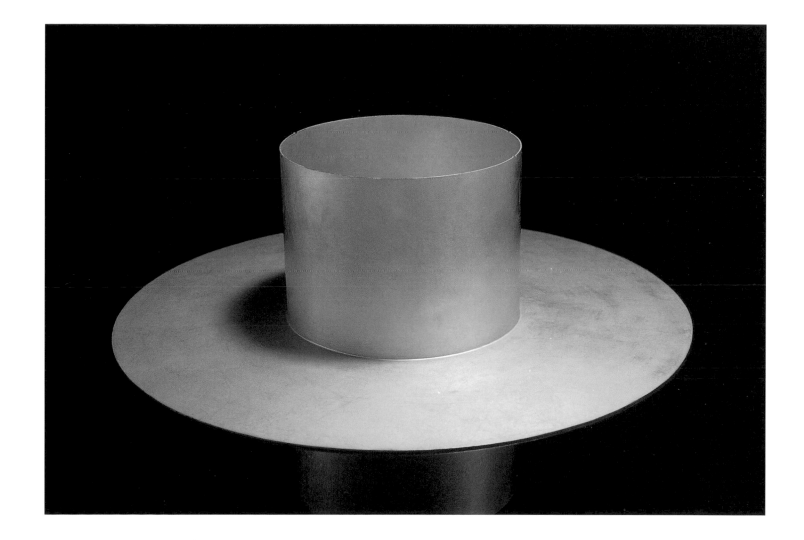

67 **Conditions for Ornament No.2,**
   Conical/Cylindrical Vessels
   1988
   Brass, tin finish
   24 x 128 x 32 cm; 9 x 50.5 x 12.5 in
   Private collection
   Photograph: David Cripps

68 **Conditions for Ornament No.3,**
Cylindrical Vessel 1988
Brass, tin finish
22 x 25.5 x 35 cm; 8.5 x 10 x 13.75 in
Private collection
Photograph: David Cripps

69 **Conditions for Ornament No.5,**
Conical Vessel 1988
Brass, gold leaf finish
26 x 24 x 34 cm; 10.25 x 9.5 x 13.75 in
Private collection
Photograph: David Cripps

opposite
70 **Conditions for Ornament No.7,**
Conical Vessel 1988
Brass, tin finish
43 x 28 x 28 cm; 17 x 11 x 11 in
Private collection
Photograph: Ian Haigh

78

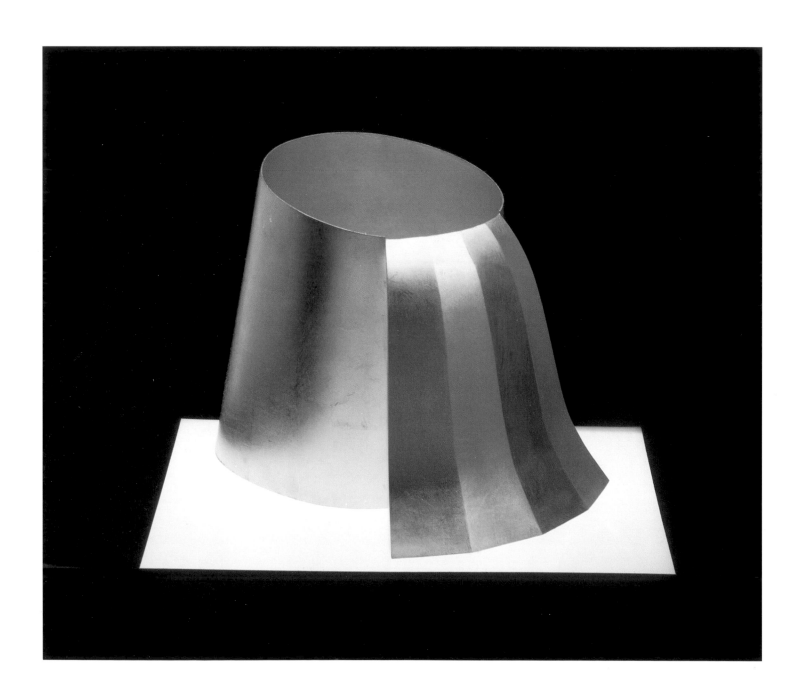

71 **Conditions for Ornament No.8,**
Conical Vessel 1988
Brass, tin finish
28 x 52 x 22 cm; 11 x 20.5 x 8.75 in
Private collection
Photograph: David Cripps

opposite
72 **Conditions for Ornament No.4,**
Double Cylindrical Vessel on
Base 1988
Brass, tin finish
51 x 56 x 30 cm; 20 x 22 x 11.75 in
Collection: Crafts Council, London
Photograph: David Cripps

80

73 **Conditions for Ornament No.11,**
Conical Vessel 1989
Brass, tin finish
30 x 40 x 26 cm; 11.75 x 15.75 x 10.2 in
Collection: 401½ Collection
Photograph: Ian Haigh

opposite
74 **Conditions for Ornament No.12,**
Conical Vessel 1990
Brass, gold leaf finish
42 x 22.5 x 40.5 cm; 16.5 x 9 x 16 in
Private collection
Photograph: Sigert Thomanetz

82

75-76 **Conditions for Ornament No.13,**
       Cubic/Conical/Cylindrical Vessel 1992
Brass, tin finish
34 x 37 x 14 cm; 13.5 x 14.5 x 5.5 in
Private collection
Photograph: David Cripps

84

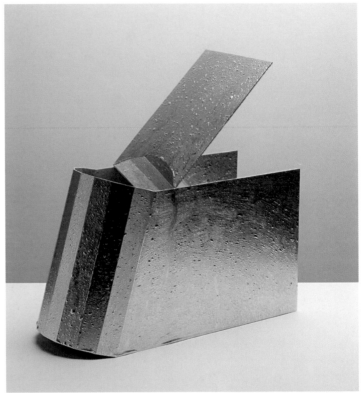

opposite
77 **Conical Vessel** 1992
Brass, tin finish
26 x 44 x 36 cm; 10.25 x 17.25 x 14 in
Private collection
Photograph: David Cripps

78 **Conditions for Ornament No.14,**
Conical Vessel 1992
Brass, tin finish
52 x 38 x 25 cm;
20.5 x 15 x 10 in
Collection: West Norway Museum of
Decorative Art, Bergen
Photograph: David Cripps

opposite
79 **Conditions for Ornament No.15,**
Conical Vessel 1992
Brass, tin finish
44 x 28 x 26 cm;
17.25 x 11 x 10.25 in
Collection: Aberdeen Art Gallery
and Museums Collections
Photograph: David Cripps

opposite
80 **Conical Vessel** 1992
Brass, gold leaf finish
38 x 31 x 28 cm; 15 x 12.25 x 11 in
Private collection
Photograph: David Cripps

81 **Conditions for Ornament No.16,
Lidded Container** 1992
Brass, brown patination
30 x 35 x 35 cm; 11.75 x 13.75 x 13.75 in
Private collection
Photograph: David Cripps

82 **Conical Vessel** 1992
Brass, brown patination
38 x 30 x 16 cm; 15 x 11.75 x 6.25 in
Private collection
Photograph: David Cripps

83 **Conical Vessel** 1993
Brass, tin finish
47 x 30 x 12 cm; 18.5 x 11.75 x 4.75 in
Collection: 401½ Collection
Photograph: David Cripps

84 **Conical Vessel** 1993
Brass, gold leaf finish
37 x 31 x 21 cm; 14.5 x 12.5 x 8.25 in
Collection: National Museum
of Modern Art, Tokyo
Photograph: David Cripps

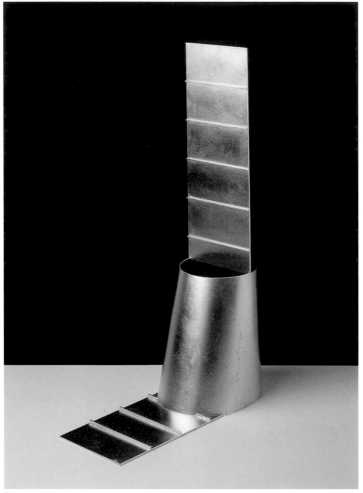

opposite
85 **Conditions for Ornament No.18,
Cylindrical Vessel** 1993
Brass, tin finish
34 x 30 x 20 cm; 13.25 x 11.75 x 8 in
Collection: Stedelijk Museum, Amsterdam
Photograph: David Cripps

86 **Conditions for Ornament No.19, Lidded Container** 1993
Brass, gold leaf finish
37 x 31 x 21 cm; 14.5 x 12.25 x 8.25 in
Private collection
Photograph: David Cripps

87 **Conditions for Ornament No.20, Lidded Container** 1993
Brass, gold leaf finish
37 x 31 x 21 cm; 14.25 x 12.25 x 8.25 in
Collection: National Museum
of Modern Art, Tokyo
Photograph: David Cripps

88 **Conditions for Ornament No.21,**
Box 1994
925 silver
16 x 28 x 6 cm; 6.25 x 11 x 2.5 in
Collection: National Museum
of Modern Art, Tokyo
Photograph: Michael Rowe

**89 Development Drawing for
Conditions for Ornament No.22 1994**
Pencil on paper
59.4 x 42 cm; 23.5 x 16.5 in
Collection: Rowe Archive

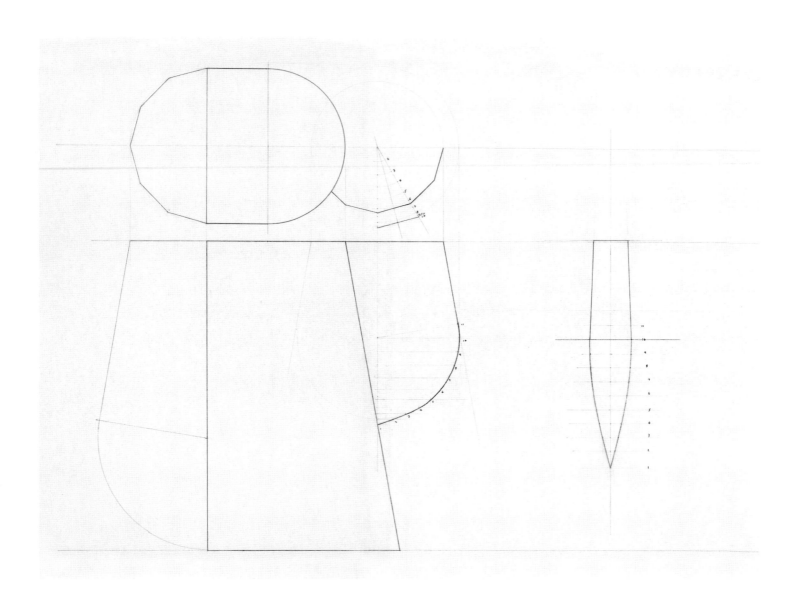

90 **Conditions for Ornament No.22,**
Conical Vessel 1994
Brass, gold leaf finish
27 x 37 x 22 cm; 10.5 x 14.5 x 8.5 in
Private collection
Photograph: David Cripps

91–92 **Conditions for Ornament No.23, Lidded Container** 1994

Brass, gold leaf finish
54 x 40 x 15 cm;
21.25 x 15.75 x 6 in
Collection: Trustees of the National
Museums of Scotland
Photograph: David Cripps

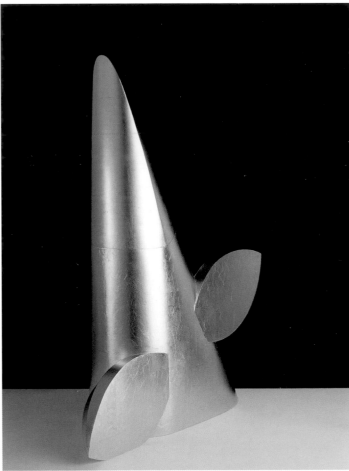

93 **Conditions for Ornament No.27,**
Conical Vase 1994

Brass, tin finish
(limited edition)
16 x 54 x 38 cm;
6.25 x 21.25 x 15 in
Collection: Museum Boymans
van Beuningen, Rotterdam
Photograph: David Cripps

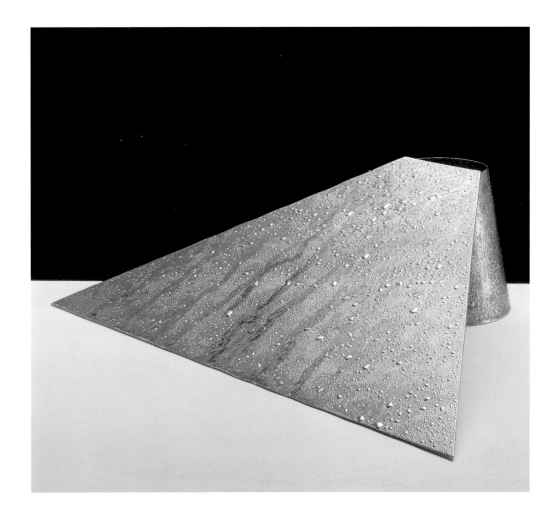

94 **Conditions for
Ornament No.24,
Conical Vessel** 1994
Brass, gold leaf finish
30 x 26 x 40 cm;
11.75 x 10 x 15.75 in
Collection: Musée des Arts
Décoratifs, Paris
Photograph: David Cripps

95 **Conditions for Ornament No.25, Conical Vase** 1994

Brass, tin finish
51 x 18.5 x 22 cm;
20 x 7.25 x 8.75 in
Private collection
Photograph: David Cripps

96 **Conditions for Ornament No.26, Conical Vase** 1994

Brass, tin finish
(limited edition)
58 x 19 x 22 cm;
22.75 x 7.5 x 8.75 in
Collection: Musée des Arts Decoratifs, Paris
Photograph: David Cripps

97 **Measured Drawing of the Silver Trust Candelabra** 1994

Ink on tracing paper

59.4 x 42 cm;

23.5 x 16.5 in

Collection: Rowe Archive

Photograph: David Bailey

98 **Pair of Candelabra** 1994

925 silver

58 x 37.5 x 37.5 cm;

22.75 x 14.75 x 14.75 in

Design: Michael Rowe

Maker: Norman Bassant

Collection: The Silver Trust Commissions for 10 Downing Street

Photograph: Alf Barnes

100

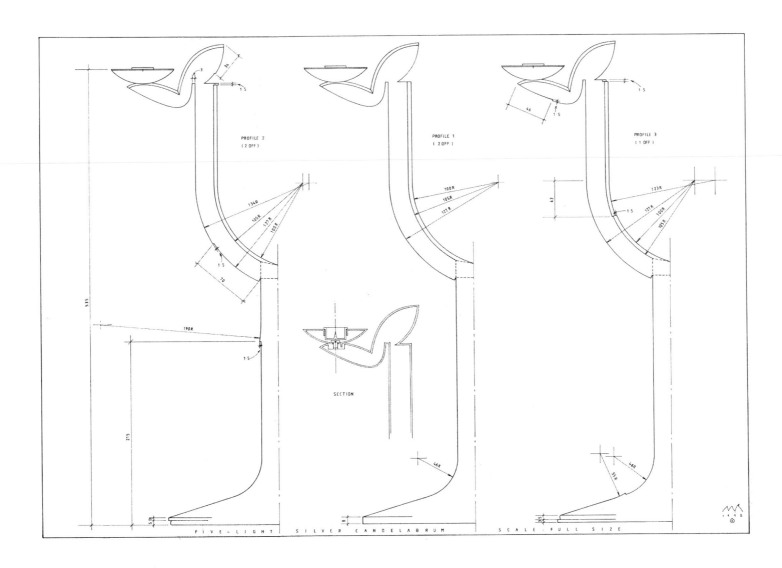

PROFILE 2 (2 OFF)   PROFILE 1 (2 OFF)   PROFILE 3 (1 OFF)

SECTION

F I V E - L I G H T   S I L V E R   C A N D E L A B R U M   S C A L E : F U L L   S I Z E

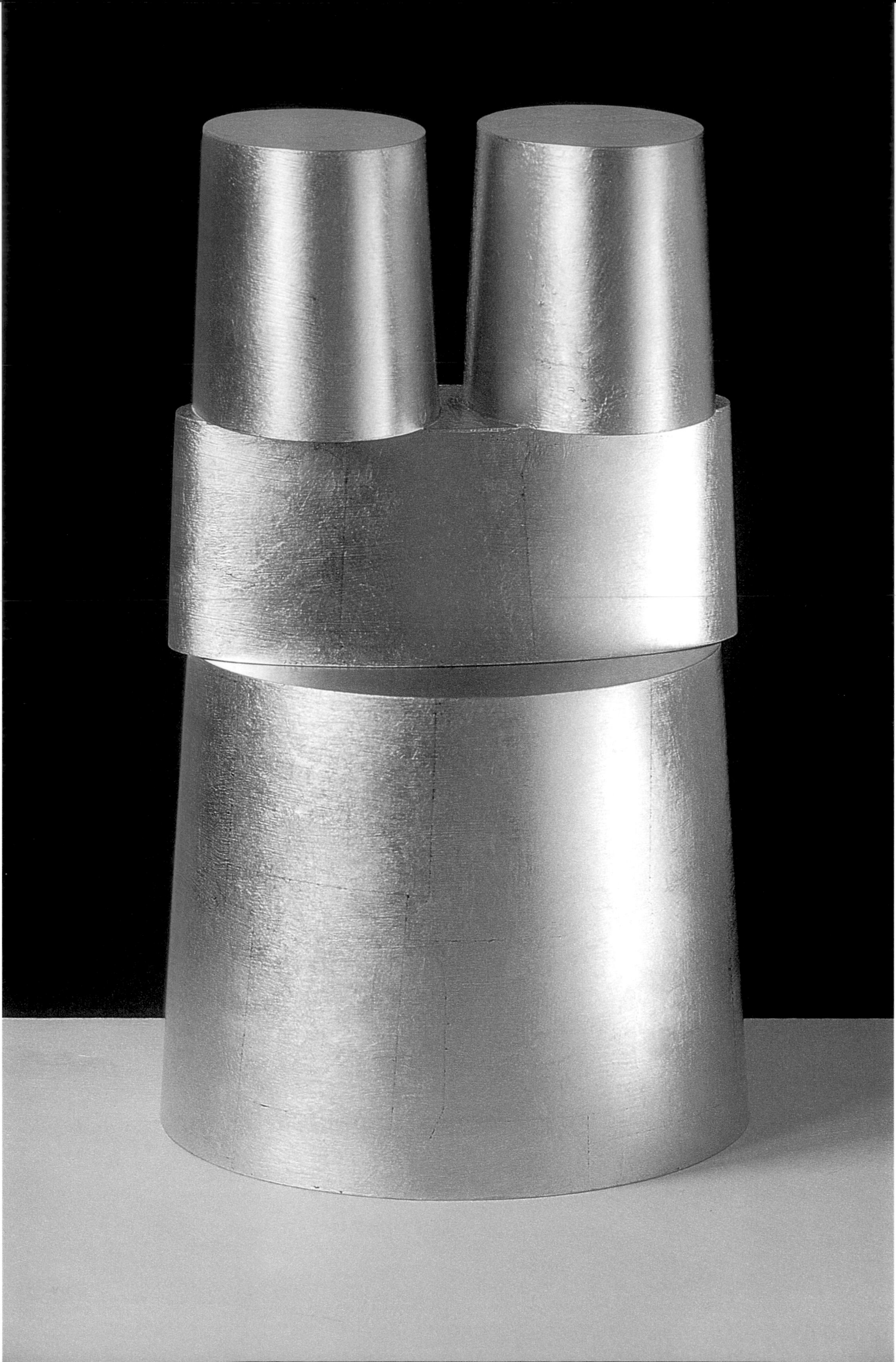

opposite

**99 Conditions for Ornament
No.28, Lidded Container**
1996
Brass, gold leaf finish
36 x 21 x 21 cm;
14 x 8.25 x 8.25 in
Collection: Purchased by the
Contemporary Art Society Special
Collection Scheme for Birmingham
Museums and Art Gallery
Photograph: David Cripps

**100 Conditions for Ornament
No.30, Cubic Vase with
Ellipses** 1999
Brass, tin finish
47.5 x 18 x 35 cm;
18.75 x 7 x 13.75 in
Private collection
Photograph: David Cripps

102 **After Euclid:**
Elliptical Bowl 2000
925 silver
11 x 18.5 x 12.5 cm;
4.25 x 7.25 x 5 in
Private collection
Photograph: David Cripps

opposite
101 **Conditions for Ornament**
No.31, Conical Vase 2000
925 silver
45 x 22 x 20 cm;
17.75 x 8.5 x 8 in
Collection: The Worshipful
Company of Goldsmiths
Photograph: Clarissa Bruce

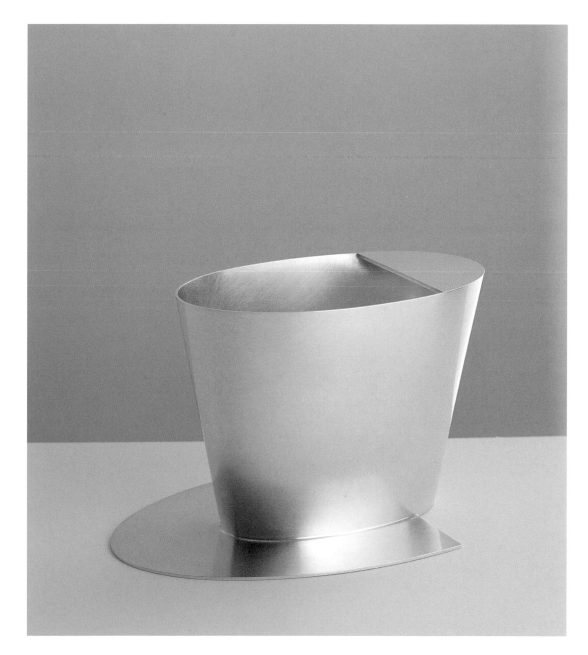

103 **After Euclid:**
Cream Jug 2001
925 silver
8 x 15.5 x 10.5 cm;
3.25 x 6 x 4.25 in
Private collection
Photograph: David Cripps

104 **After Euclid:**
Small Jug 2001
925 silver
14 x 17 x 11.5 cm;
5.5 x 6.75 x 4.5 in
Private collection
Photograph: David Cripps

105 **After Euclid:**
Cup 2002
925 silver
14.5 x 9 x 9.5 cm;
5.75 x 3.5 x 3.75 in
Commissioned by Sheffield Assay
Office as part of the Millennium
Cup Project
Photograph: Michael Harvey

106 **After Euclid:**
Drawing for Cream Jug 2002
Pencil on paper
29.7 x 21 cm; 11.75 x 8.25 in
Collection: Rowe Archive

107 **After Euclid:**
Cream Jug 2002
925 silver
11 x 17 x 8.5 cm; 4.25 x 6.75 x 3.5 in
Private collection
Photograph: David Cripps

108 **After Euclid:**
Small Serving Plate 2003
925 silver
3 x 17.5 x 15 cm; 1.25 x 7 x 7 in
Private collection
Photograph: Michael Harvey

110

109 **After Euclid:**
Fish Server 2002
925 silver
7 x 31 x 12 cm;
2.75 x 12.25 x 4.75 in
Private collection
Photograph: Michael Harvey

110 **After Euclid:**
Elliptical Bowl 2000
925 silver
12 x 18 x 12.5 cm ; 4.75 x 7 x 5 in
Private collection
Photograph: David Cripps

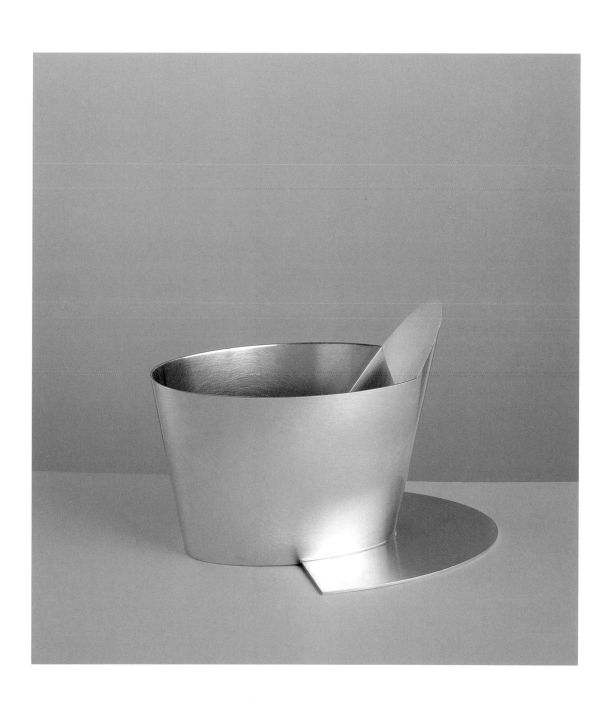

112 **Cornerwork:**
Night and Day 2003
925 silver
34 x 33 x 20 cm;
13.25 x 13 x 8 in
Private collection
Photograph: Michael Harvey

111 **After Euclid:**
Cornerwork 2003
925 silver
15 x 32 x 23 cm;
6 x 12.5 x 9 in
Private collection
Photograph: Michael Harvey

overleaf left
113 **After Euclid:**
Cornerwork 2003
925 silver
40 x 20.5 x 12 cm;
15.75 x 8 x 4.75 in
Private collection
Photograph: Michael Harvey

overleaf right
114 **After Euclid:**
Cornerwork 2003
925 silver
11 x 37 x 9 cm;
4.25 x 14.5 x 3.5 in
Private collection
Photograph: Michael Harvey

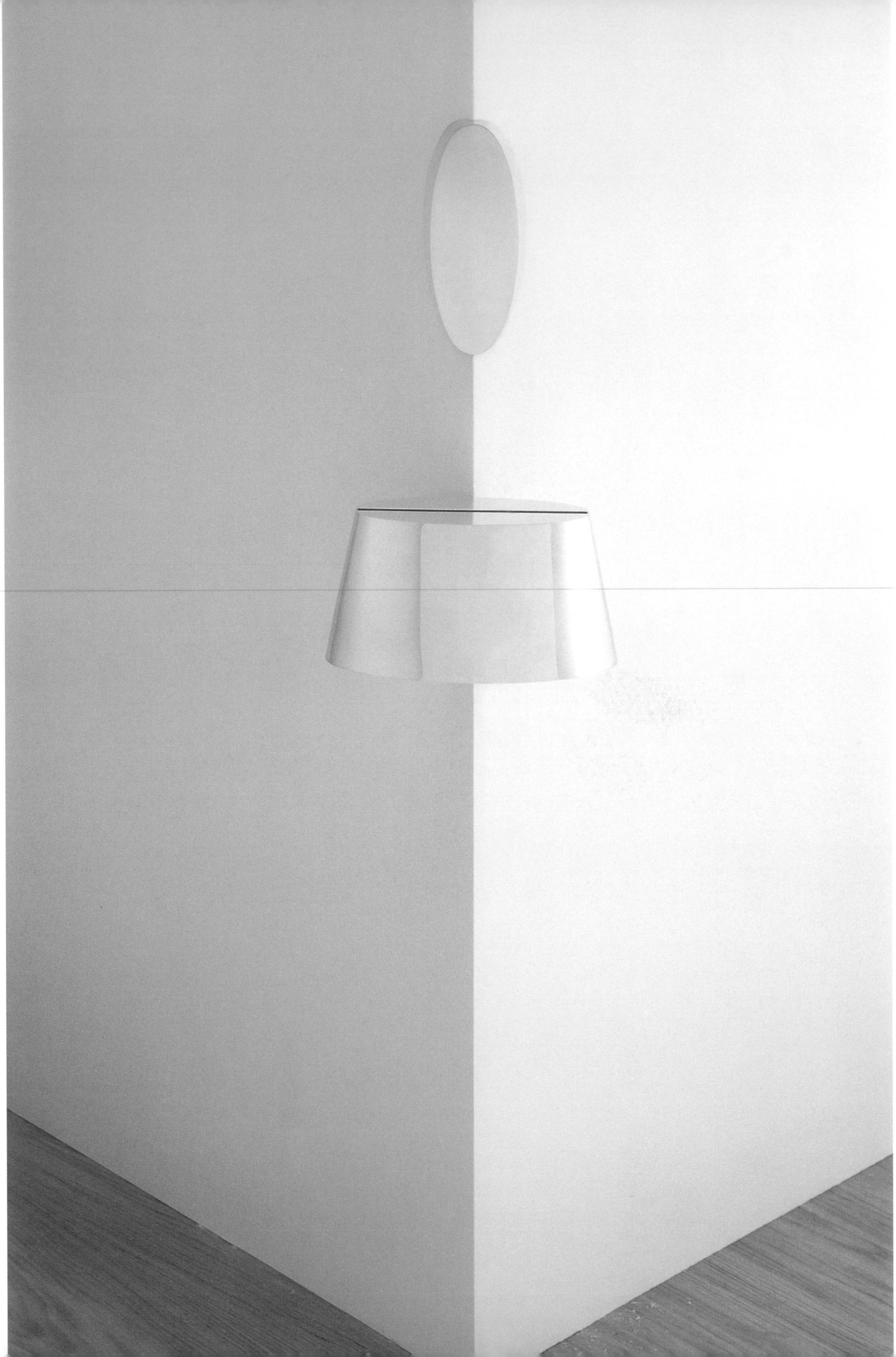

Chronology

1948 Born, High Wycombe, Buckinghamshire, England

1959 High Wycombe Technical High School: First Metalwork

1965–6 High Wycombe College of Technology and Art: Foundation Course

1966–9 High Wycombe College, Dip.AD, First Class Honours in Silversmithing Design

1967 Awarded Frogmoor Foundation Travelling Scholarship

1969–72 Royal College of Art, MA in Silversmithing and Jewellery

1971–2 Sunglass designs for Polaroid UK Limited

1972 Set up studio at 401½ Workshops, London

1972 First gallery exhibition: group summer show at Electrum Gallery, London

1973 Spectacle designs for Optical Information Council fashion promotion

1973–82 Visiting lecturer, Buckinghamshire College of Higher Education

1974 Awarded Diploma of the World Crafts Council
Awarded Crafts Council Setting-Up Grant

1974–6 Spectacle designs for Merx International Optical Company

1976–82 Visiting lecturer, Camberwell College of Arts and Design

1977 Produced the first of the series of silver, copper and brass boxes

1978–80 Visiting lecturer, Royal College of Art

1978–82 Research award with Richard Hughes for research into the patination and colouring of metals at Camberwell College of Arts and Design

1979– Began the series of silver and copper and patinated brass bowls

1980–4 Tutor, Royal College of Art

1982 Publication of *The Colouring, Bronzing and Patination of Metals* and associated exhibition, toured by the Crafts Council to 15 museums and art galleries in Britain

1982–5 Research with Richard Hughes into ancient patinated surfaces for the British Museum

1982– Numerous consultancy services advising on the applications of patinated finishes in architecture and design

1983 Began series of cylindrical vessels, using increasingly complex surface finishes and patination; introduced a gold leaf finish and a tinned finish from 1983

1983 Elected a Freeman of the Worshipful Company of Goldsmiths
Awarded the Freedom of the City of London
Jury member for *Das Tablett* international silver design competition organised by the Gesellschaft für Goldschmiedekunst, Hanau
Lectured at art academies in Düsseldorf, Cologne, Schwabisch-Gmund, Pforzheim and Munich

1984– Course leader/Senior tutor, Royal College of Art

1984 Project leader, Rietveld Akademie, Amsterdam
Met his partner, the metal artist Iene Ambar

1985 Project leader, College of Art and Crafts, Oslo
Speaker, SNAG Conference, Toronto, Canada

1986 Speaker, JMGA Conference, Perth, Australia.
Also lectured at the Meat Market Art Centre, Melbourne

1987 Began the *Conditions for Ornament* series
Gulbenkian Foundation *Vessel Forum*: speaker at Birmingham followed by *Vessel Workshop* at West Sussex College of Art and Design; created series of bronze/iron pieces working in the College foundry
Elected Fellow of the Royal College of Art
Project leader, with Richard Hughes, at Bezalel College of Art, Jerusalem

1988 Winner, Sotheby's Decorative Arts Award

1989 Elected Fellow of the Royal Society of Arts

1991 Project leader and speaker at Harbourfront Arts Centre, Toronto
Lectured at Rhode Island School of Design, Providence, USA
Lectured to new silversmiths' group, *Silber in Beweging*, Vakskool, Schoonhoven, Holland
Speaker at *Haldenhof'91* Symposium, Wissgoldingen, Germany

1992 Jury member for the international exhibition *European Contemporary Silverwork: Een Schiterend Feest*, Brussels

1993 Member of the selection committee and text contributor to the catalogue for the exhibition, *Twentieth Century Silver*, Crafts Council, London
Speaker, *The Silver Symposium*, Victoria and Albert Museum, London
Awarded an Artist's Fellowship by the Japan Foundation
Lectured extensively in Japan, including the Tokyo National University of Fine Arts and Music

1995 Speaker, *First International Metal Arts Symposium*, Won-Kwang University, Iksan, South Korea
Speaker, *Japanese Studio Crafts Symposium*, Victoria and Albert Museum, London

1996 Began work on conic sections and the ellipse series, *After Euclid*
Speaker, *Contemporary Silver Symposium*, Victoria and Albert Museum, London

1998 Awarded Second Prize in the *European Prize for Contemporary Art and Design* organised by the World Crafts Council (Europe)
Interview with Irena Goldscheider of the Prague Museum for the Decorative Arts published in the catalogue of the *Metalmorphosis* exhibition

1993 *Worum geht's? Ausstellung in funf Sequenzen*, Roemer-Pelizaeus Museum, Hildesheim, Germany

1993 *Twentieth Century Silver*, Crafts Council, London and touring

1993 *The Chemistry Set*, Crafts Council, London and touring

1994 *'Metallgefasse', Form und Funktion im Wechselspiel*, Galerie für Angewandte Kunst, Munich, Germany

1994 *'Korpus': Norsk Kunsthandwerk 1994*, Vestlandske Kunstindustrimuseum, Bergen, Norway

1994 *The National Collection: The Silver Trust Commissions*, Goldsmiths' Hall, London, 1994, and subsequent tours

1995 *Petersburger Hangung*, Galerie Spectrum, Munich, Germany

1995 *Handmade: Changing Taste in the Look of the Crafts*, Walker Art Gallery, Liverpool

1996 *Design of the Times: 100 Years of the Royal College of Art*, RCA, London

1996 *First Choice*, Museum Boymans van Beuningen, Rotterdam, The Netherlands

1996-8 *Objects of Our Time*, Silver Jubilee Exhibition of the Crafts Council, Crafts Council, London and touring

1997-8 *Design mit Zukunft* (curated by Philippe Starke), Focke Museum, Bremen and Museum für Angewandte Kunst, Cologne, Germany

1997-8 *The RCA School of Applied Arts*, Museum für Kunst und Gewerbe, Hamburg, and touring to Kassel and Munich, Germany

1998 *Beyond Material*, Oriel Mostyn, Llandudno and touring

1998-9 *European Prize for Contemporary Art and Design-Led Crafts*, World Crafts Council (Europe), Palais Harrach, Vienna, Austria, and touring to Rohsska Museum, Gothenburg, Sweden, Musée des Arts Decoratifs, Paris, France and VIZO Gallery, Brussels, Belgium

1998-9 *Metalmorphosis: British Silver and Metalwork 1880-1998*, British Council and the Museum of Decorative Arts, Prague, Czech Republic, and touring to the Brohan Museum, Berlin, Germany

1999 *World Contemporary Craft Now*, Cheongju International Craft Biennale, Cheongju Arts Centre, Cheongju, South Korea

2000 *Treasures of the Twentieth Century*, Goldsmiths' Hall, London

2000 *Three Decades: Objects Selected From the Crafts Council Collection, 1972-99*, The London Institute Gallery, London

2001 *Fortuna: Tempus Fugit*, Bomuldsfabriken Galleri-Kunstsammling, Arendal, Norway

2001 *Metallit 2001*, Fiskarsin Kuparipaja, Fiskars, Finland

2001 *Cheongju Second International Craft Biennale*, invitational exhibition, Cheongju Arts Centre, Cheongju, South Korea

2002 *Masterpieces*, centenary exhibition of modern decorative art, Palazzo Bricherasio, Turin, Italy

Selected commissions

1972   Crafts Council: a silver pomander (1973) for *The Craftsman's Art* exhibition at the Victoria and Albert Museum

1975   Liberty & Co: a silver pomander for their *Centenary* exhibition at the Victoria and Albert Museum (now lost)

1980   West Midlands Arts: a silver and copper bowl, subsequently presented to Birmingham Museum and Art Gallery

1994   The Silver Trust: a pair of silver candelabra for No.10 Downing Street

1997   The Worshipful Company of Goldsmiths: a silver vase for the permanent collection

2002   Sheffield Assay Office: a cup for the Millennium Cup project

Public collections

Australia
Art Gallery of Western Australia, Perth

France
Musée des Arts Décoratifs, Paris

Germany
Badisches Landesmuseum, Karlsruhe

Italy
Museum of Applied Arts, Turin

Japan
National Museum of Modern Art, Tokyo

The Netherlands
Museum Boymans van Beuningen, Rotterdam
Stedelijk Museum, Amsterdam

Norway
Nordenfjeldske Kunstindustrimuseum, Trondheim
Vestlandske Kunstindustrimuseum, Bergen

United Kingdom
Aberdeen Art Gallery
Birmingham Museums and Art Gallery
Crafts Council Collection, London
Leeds City Art Gallery
Royal Museum of Scotland, Edinburgh
Shipley Art Gallery, Gateshead
Victoria and Albert Museum, London
Worshipful Company of Goldsmiths, London

Selected bibliography

Beaumont-Nesbitt, Brian, 'New silversmiths', *Architectural Review*, September, 1974

Bellini, Mario (ed.), *The International Design Yearbook, 1990–1*, Thames & Hudson, London, 1990

Berkum, Ans van, 'Michael Rowe: A taste for simplicity', *Bijvoorbeeld* (The Netherlands), January 1994

Blair, Claude, *The History of Silver*, Macdonald Orbis, London, 1987

Bond, D'Este, 'Michael Rowe, silversmith', *Crafts*, March 1973

Bragg, Craig-Martin, Frayling et al., *Vision: 50 Years of British Creativity*, Thames & Hudson, London, 1999

Brittain, Judy, 'Michael Rowe's treasure chest', *Vogue*, June 1974

Britton, Alison, 'The four tops: Modern classics', *Art Review*, vol.XLVI, December/January 1995

Coatts, Margot, 'Sources of inspiration: Michael Rowe', *Crafts*, January/February 2003

Cooper, Emmanuel, 'Michael Rowe', *Art & Artists*, February 1979

Crafts Council, *The Crafts Council Collection, 1972–85*, Crafts Council, London, 1985

'Design work of Michael Rowe', *Portfolio Design Magazine* (Japan), August 1990

Destefan, Fabio, 'Michael Rowe: Poetry in the shape of things', *Forme* (Italy), no.149, March 1993

Dormer, Peter (ed.), *The Illustrated Dictionary of Twentieth Century Designers*, Quarto, London, 1991

Ellis, Martin, 'Michael Rowe', *Goldsmiths' Review*

2002/2003, Worshipful Company of Goldsmiths, London, 2003

Evans, James, 'Michael Rowe', *Kunsthandverk* (Norway), no.54, March 1994

First International Metal Arts Symposium, conference report, Won-Kwang University, Ik San, Korea, 1995

Forskning og Kunstnerisk Utviklingsarbeid Innen Kunstfagene, report, University of Oslo, 1995

Frayling, Christopher, *Art & Design: 100 Years of the Royal College of Art*, RCA, London, 1999

Frost, Abigail, 'Conditions for ornament', *Design Week*, October 1988

Goldscheider, Irena, 'Interview with Michael Rowe', *Metalmorphosis*, exh.cat., Museum of Decorative Arts, Prague and the British Council, London, 1998

Goodison, Sir Nicholas, 'The crafts and their industrial future', *Royal Society of Arts Journal*, vol.CXLV, 1998

Harrod, Tanya, *The Crafts in Britain in the 20th Century*, Yale University Press, New Haven and London, 1999

Hill, Rosemary, 'Containing genius: The grammar of ornament in Michael Rowe's vessels', *Crafts*, January 1989

Hughes, Richard and Rowe, Michael, 'Patination: The chemical colouring of metals', *Crafts*, September 1982

Hughes, Richard and Rowe, Michael, *The Colouring, Bronzing and Patination of Metals*, Crafts Council, London, 1982, reissued by Thames & Hudson, London, 1991 and Watson-Guptill/Whitney Library of Design, New York, 1991

Huygen, Frederique, *British Design: Image & Identity*, Thames & Hudson, London, 1989

Joppien, Rudiger, 'Europaïsches Silberschmiede', *Kunst und Handwerk* (Germany), January 1986

Joppien, Rudiger, *'Metallgefasse', Form and Funktion im Wechselspiel,* Galerie für Angewandte Kunst, Munich, 1994

Lee, Hye Won, 'Michael Rowe', *Arts & Crafts* (Korea), no.11, 1992

Loyen, Frances, *Silversmithing*, Thames & Hudson, London, 1980

Margetts, Martina, *International Crafts*, Thames & Hudson, London, 1991

Margetts, Martina, 'Things Gather World' in *Michael Rowe* exh.cat., Museum für Angewandte Kunst, Cologne, Germany, 1992

Margetts, Martina, 'Metalwork and Metamorphosis' in *The Chemistry Set* exh.cat., Crafts Council, London, 1993

Mendini, Alessandro (ed.), *The International Design Yearbook, 1996*, Calmann & King, London, 1996

'Michael Rowe: Objects in metal', *Goldsmiths' Journal* (USA), December 1978

Norton, Deborah, 'Michael Rowe: A Conversation with Deborah Norton', *Metalsmith* (USA), vol.9, no.3, 1989

Park, Inn-Soek, *Nouvel Objet 2*, Design House, Seoul, Korea, 1997

Paz, Octavio and Plant, James, *In Praise of Hands*, New York Graphic Society, New York, 1974

Putman, Andrée (ed.), *The International Design Yearbook, 1991-2*, Thames & Hudson, London, 1991

Radziewksy, Elke von, 'Where form is an enigma', *Architektur und Wohnen* (Germany), April/May, 1987

Ramshaw, Wendy, 'Attacking the basic forms: The work of Michael Rowe', *Art Aurea* (Germany), April 1992

Reid, Christopher, 'Isoblique boxes: The new work of Michael Rowe', *Crafts*, January 1979

Rowe, Michael, 'Contrasting pieces', in *Our Domestic Landscape*, exh.cat., Cornerhouse Arts Centre, Manchester, 1987

Rowe, Michael, 'Inheriting Modernism', in *20th Century Silver*, exh.cat., Crafts Council, London, 1993

Rowe, Michael, 'Contemporary metalwork', contribution to the article 'Taking stock', *Crafts*, March/April 1994

'Six metalsmith masters visit Korea', *Design Monthly* (Korea), vol.204, June 1995

Starke, Philippe (ed.), *The International Design Yearbook 1987-8*, Thames & Hudson, London, 1987

Starke, Philippe (ed.), *The International Design Yearbook 1997*, Calmann & King, London, 1997

van der Meijden, Peter, 'Denken door te doen: de "bevatters" van Michael Rowe', *Km Magazine*, Amsterdam, no.44, Winter 2002

Acknowledgements

It is a rare thing for museums to be given the opportunity to engage in collaborations that extend their range and broaden their horizons. *Show5* is just such a collaboration, and Birmingham Museums and Art Gallery owes considerable thanks to Louise Taylor of the Crafts Council for initiating the project. I am also grateful to my fellow *Show5* curators: Louise Clark at the Crafts Council, Lucien Cooper at Stoke, Kate Day at Manchester, Mark Prest at Leicester and my colleague Zelina Garland at Birmingham for their encouragement, commitment to shared ideals and good companionship.

At Lund Humphries, I should like to thank Nigel Farrow and Lucy Clark for their brave embracing of our ambitious and demanding proposal for the publication of all of the *Show5* books as a series. Alison Green's sympathetic project management has brought orchestrated order to our huge and unwieldy enterprise. In the production of this book, I am very grateful to Simon Perry for his support, painstaking editing and coordination, and to Chrissie Charlton for her understanding, patience and wonderful design. The new photography undertaken by David Cripps, Michael Harvey and David Bailey has provided an invaluable resource and we are immensely grateful to all of the owners whose works are reproduced here, whether private individuals or institutions, for their assistance and generosity.

Martina Margetts's and Richard Hill's excellent and insightful essays cast new light on Rowe's work, and provide the broader cultural contexts of philosophy, architecture and geometry which it demands. But above all, my thanks are due to Michael Rowe for his vision, dedication and inspirational presence in the development of this publication and the major exhibition of his work, organised by Birmingham Museums and Art Gallery, with which its production coincides. It is a project in which we are privileged to have been involved.

Martin Ellis
Curator (Applied Art), Department of Art
Birmingham Museums and Art Gallery

Index of works